# This Great Awakening

## The part we all play in this time of our lives

By Eileen McCourt

# This Great Awakening

## The part we all play in this time of our lives

### By Eileen McCourt

# Contents

**PART THREE: AWAKENING TO WHO YOU REALLY ARE**

**PART FOUR: AWAKENING TO THE TRUE
UNDERSTANDING OF THE TEACHINGS OF CHRIST**

**EPILOGUE:**

# About the Author

Eileen McCourt is a graduate of University College Dublin, with a Master's degree in History. She is a retired professional school teacher of English and History.

She is a Reiki Grand Master Teacher, teaching the following to all levels:

- Usui Reiki

- Rahanni Celestial Healing

- Fire Spirit Reiki  (Christ Consciousness and Holy Spirit)

- Archangels Reiki

- The Violet Flame

- Mother Mary Reiki

- Unicorn

- Dolphin

- Dragon

- Elementals

- Golden Eagle (Native American)

- Psychic Surgery

Eileen is also a fully qualified Master Practitioner of the following: Okuna Reiki (Atlantean and Lemurian); Lemurian Crystal;  Tera-Mai Reiki Seichem; Pegasus; Golden Rainbow Ray;  Golden Chalice; Goddess of Light.

She has qualified in Ireland, England and Spain; in England through the Lynda Bourne School of Enlightenment; in Spain, through the Spanish

Federation of Reiki with Allessandra Rossin, Bienestar, Santa Eulalia, Ibiza.

Eileen lives in Warrenpoint, County Down, Northern Ireland. She has travelled extensively throughout the world.

She is currently working on her third book: "Working With Spirit: Healing for Our Times."

Her first book, "Living the Magic" was published in December 2014

She has also recorded several guided Meditation cd's, accompanied by her brother, Pianist Pat McCourt:

"Celestial Healing"

"Celestial Presence"

"Chakra Cleansing, Energising and Balancing"

"Ethereal Spirit"

"Open the Door to Archangel Michael"

The list of outlets for books and cd's is to be found on Eileen's website: www.celestialhealing8.co.uk

Her e-mail address, should anyone wish to contact her, is: celestialhealing8@yahoo.co.uk

**Eileen's previous book 'Living the Magic' is available via Amazon. ISBN: 978-1503205024**

Reclining Buddha in Shanghai, China.

Temple offerings in Bali

Quan yin the Jade Temple, Shanghai, China.

# ACKNOWLEDGEMENTS

I wish to express my sincere and deep appreciation to the following:

Margaret Hurdman, for her continued support, guidance and friendship;

My family and friends, both those in this incarnation and those in Spirit, for their constant encouragement, and for their unfailing faith in me;

My publishers, Don Hale OBE and Dr Steve Green for their contributions;

The staff at Mourne Office Supplies, Warrenpoint, especially Bronagh, Emma, Trish, Sarah. They truly are the wind beneath my wings!

All those beautiful people in the Angel shops and Holistic centres around the country: Janet and Stephen in Angel Times, Limerick; Niamh and David in Elements, Galway; Mairead Murray in Dreamcatchers, Cavan; Helen, Valerie, Mary Rose in Blue Moon, Derry; Shane, Claire and Colleen in Elysium, Newry; Tony and Trish Doyle in Tricia's Angel Shop, Arklow; Margaret Deacon, Angelic Companions, Gorey; Christine in Crysalis, Belfast; Bridget Price, Rainbow Healing, Carlow; Mary Queeney, Healing Earth, Galway; Angela and Jay, Angels with Dirty Faces, Ballyfermot; John and Deborah in Deborah's Country Café, Nenagh; Sinead Coleman, Purple Lotus, New Ross; Patricia, Stephen and Kim in Angels of Ireland, Ashbourne.

We are truly so blessed to have all these centres! These people are not just there to sell Angel figurines or whatever. They are Beacons of Light, holding the Divine Energy in their own area, spiralling it outwards, offering a helping hand to all of us along our way. They are the feet on the ground for Spirit. The best favour that you can do for yourself is to connect with the centre nearest you; there you will find courses, workshops, therapies, healings, all the help and support you need as you continue on your own Spiritual journey. You are never alone; these people are here to help,-that is what they do!

A very special thank you, too, to all those who have bought my books and cd's, and who have attended my workshops, courses and healing sessions. It is all of you who make my work so worth-while!

Most of all, thank you Spirit, for all the abundance and amazing gifts with which You flood my life, and for the constant synchronicities that remind me that I am never alone, but always being looked after by a Greater Force that knows all my needs, and provides for them. For all the gifts and blessings showered on me each and every day, I am truly grateful!

Eileen McCourt

September 4th 2015

# REVIEWS

"A most comprehensive book on Spiritual Awakening. This book is written in an honest and soul-searching way to which spiritual people will relate. The author has explored old beliefs in spirituality and brought it all into the twenty- first century. An enjoyable and well worth read."

Lynda Bourne, School of Enlightenment, West Midlands.

"An informative and descriptive book that flows with a sincerity of modern and historical spiritual realism. Partly autobiographical in nature, the author has vividly sought and achieved an integration of spiritual knowledge with facets of her own experience.
This book is a benchmark in generic consciousness which will reverberate for many years. A terrific read!"

Clare Bowman, Spiritual Historian

"This book is a no-nonsense book. It holds the key to many thoughts that have not been put into words before. Very enlightening!
I applaud the levels of understanding regarding fact, fiction and the need for truth. All religions at all times have fear of the unknown about them. When we trust our own self, we can understand our need to question and find ourselves,- who we are, why we are and the purpose of our being. Life is a challenge. Our reason for our being is to grow and discover our Spiritual Self. This book is a good step into the Enlightenment of ourselves."

Margaret Hurdman, Spiritual Medium.

Eileen Mc Court is capable of bringing wonderment to all   This exciting book  on awakening helps us to open  our hearts and souls  and to understand who we are. And why we are here. It is beautifully written.

Francesca Brown

In 'The Great Awakening', Eileen McCourt has given us an essential understanding of a uniquely personal, yet universal, spiritual journey. From her own experience, Eileen has found that, gone are the days of deferring to dusty, control-based 'authority' figures on our way to divine understanding. Real, flesh and blood spirituality in the 21st Century speaks of the freshness and growth of personal contact with Spirit. Without the use of contrived, 'New Age-isms', Eileen presents her own life experience and journey as a model for spiritual change, not to replicate, but to inspire.
The Great Awakening also offers the reader a practical companion on their spiritual road, bringing the topic to life with clear and concise exercises and meditations that promotes a more 'hands on' participation. This work is all about 'taking responsibility' for one's own personal and spiritual development...about time!!
Given its breadth and scope, undoubtedly this book will become an invaluable resource for all levels of spiritual seeker, from those at 'entry level', to those with more advanced understandings.
Eileen's perspective is simple, straightforward, yet significantly insightful. An important addition to the literature on the awakening consciousness.

Declan Quigley of Anam Nasca - Spiritual author and Shamanic Practitioner

# Foreword

How wondrous, how exciting, how challenging are these times in which we are living! Special times, indeed!

At this particular point, in the ongoing, unending evolution of the Cosmos, a major spiritual awakening is taking place; a seismic shift is occurring in spiritual consciousness, with astronomical changes throughout all of humanity; a Great Awakening, so profound that even those of us in the deepest of slumbers are beginning to feel the unsettling stirrings within ourselves. We are awakening to a new awareness: an awareness of our own spiritual identity; an awareness of our own inherent Divine Essence; and an awareness of our own indissoluble connection with All That Is. Like the butterfly from the cocoon, we too are metamorphosing, as we begin to remember what we have always known; as we begin to decode what has been embedded in our soul, in our own Higher Self, for aeons and aeons of time.

We are now awakening to a reclaiming of our own power, with the realisation that we ourselves have all the answers, in our own inner knowing, to all the questions we could ever ask.

We are all, each and every one of us, without exception, on the great cosmic escalator, moving rapidly towards a new glorious higher dimension for Planet Earth. There is no escaping, there is no avoiding, there is no denying our own evolutionary process. We are, of course, all at different stages on that evolutionary path, all on different levels on the upward moving escalator, but the road ahead is taking us all in the same direction, back to Source, from whence we have come. We can accept it or not; we can fight against it or go with the flow; but if we struggle against the flow, all we are doing is making the onward journey fraught with difficulties and hardships. Going with the flow, trusting that the Universal Energy knows all our requirements, guarantees, promises, ensures a joyful, happy, fulfilling experience here on Planet Earth, as each of us fulfils our own unique role in raising our own, and the collective spiritual consciousness of all humanity.

Make no mistake: Planet Earth is ascending to a higher spiritual vibration. The clarion call has gone out, and numerous souls amongst us are responding to that call. The fact that you have been drawn to this book, is a clear indication that you, too, have heard that call, and are ready to fulfil your role in this wonderful spiritual process, This Great Awakening.

We have all chosen to incarnate on this Planet Earth, at this particular point in time, to play our part, to assist in this Great Awakening. Each one of us has a unique part to play, the part for which we volunteered, the part for which we willingly signed up. No one else can play our part for us, and, equally, we cannot play the part of anyone else. Once you yourself accept your own unique role in this lifetime, once you start to go with the flow of Universal Energy, once you open up to Divine Spirit, synchronicities will flood your existence, as they have mine, healing you at a deep level and leading you onwards through your own unique role in This Great Awakening.

I invite you to let this book guide you to a recognition, to an understanding and to an acceptance of who you really are, through an awareness of your own particular soul type, and to a remembering of the part you have been called upon to play; and what we all must do to move humanity to a higher spiritual vibration, in this, our unavoidable process of collective spiritual evolution.

In this book, I explain how our history books need to be rewritten, as long-held, controlling religious dogmas and beliefs instilled into us through our education systems, give way to our own inherent knowing and mystical insights, letting our own intuition and spiritual practice direct us on our path through this lifetime.

We are also awakening to a deeper understanding of the true meanings of the teachings of Christ when He walked upon this earth. I have elaborated on six of these teachings; six teachings which I feel are so particularly relevant for us now in This Great Awakening process, this global transformation, as we awaken from the long period of detachment and forgetting from where we have come, and begin our return journey back to remembering we are all one, we are all Divine Essence, and we are all, collectively, returning to Source.

The exercises that I have included will, I hope, heighten your awareness of This Great Awakening process, helping you strengthen your connection to Divine Energy and embrace, with joy, your own beautiful, wondrous, magnificent Higher Self, your own powerful I Am Presence, as you feel and accept your deep connection to All That Is, bringing you a life of joy and wonder at all that is now unfolding before us, in This Great awakening.

As in my previous book "Living the Magic", I now ask you, once again, to step outside the comfort zone of your long-held beliefs; outside the confines of controlling institutions, enclosed societal thinking, ideologies, theologies, absolutes, the notions of right and wrong that have been instilled into you; and allow your own unique Spiritual Essence, your Soul, to fly freely, liberated from fear, unchained and unshackled, to follow its own glorious intuitive path, free from manipulation; to soar, as it was meant to soar, as you recognise your own soul type and remember the role you have undertaken to play in This Great Awakening.

So let your light shine forth, as you move forwards, without fear, to fulfil your pre-birth agreement, to help raise the collective spiritual consciousness, in this most exciting and challenging of times in which we now find ourselves, this time of Soul Ascension for you and for all humanity.

With all my love, I wish you joy and happiness as you continue on this, your earthly journey. May Spirit bless each and every one of you and may the Angels always surround you and walk with you on this, your own onward path towards Enlightenment.

I send you Love and Light!

Namaste!

Eileen McCourt

September 4<sup>th</sup> 2015

# PART ONE:  GOD UNMASKED

## Chapter One

## The God of My Childhood

Frightening, punishing, despotic. That was the image of God instilled into me during my primary school days in the 1950's.

 The God I grew up with was inaccessible, remote and severe; omnipotent, omniscient and omnipresent. He sat on a magnificent throne all the time, in Heaven, somewhere up beyond the clouds; a big man with a long flowing white beard, surrounded by the Angels and Saints. He was constantly occupied with weighing up souls on the judgement scales, to ascertain whether they were destined for upwards to Heaven, downwards to Hell or sideways to Purgatory or Limbo.

Purgatory was only a temporary sojourn, where souls were purified in flames before finally being admitted through the Pearly Gates. Hell and Limbo were permanent residing places, terrifying prospects for those souls who failed to impress at the point of entry to the After-life. Being poked at by red hot devils with piercing horns and forks was the gloomy scenario awaiting all those who fell short of the required criteria for Heaven, and condemned to Hell for all eternity.

There was no way out of Hell. A one-way street; an everlasting death sentence; burning in flames for all eternity, stretching out into infinity, with no reprise, no appeal, not able to contact God to beg forgiveness or argue your case. Not even a drink of water! You had been granted your one chance at life, and you had blown it!  Big time! Tough! No appeal, no second chance. Very tough!

Limbo was also designated as an eternal place of deprivation,- deprivation of ever seeing God. But there was a different stigma attached to Limbo. Limbo was reserved exclusively for infants who died without getting baptised. This included the still-born and the aborted. Talk about punishing the innocent!

Our religious beliefs were based on the Catechism, a series of questions and answers which had to be learned off by heart and memorised, word for word, and woe betide anyone who forgot or even stumbled over an answer! A wrong word could result in you being denied your First Holy Communion, or your Confirmation. That was the long-term punishment. And the immediate punishment? Slap, slap, slap! Thump, thump, thump! Everything seemed to be beaten into us, our fear of punishment being our only motivation for learning anything.

I remember the first question in the Catechism: "Who is God?" And the answer? "God is our Father who lives in Heaven". That was it! No mention of Him being anywhere else; just in Heaven, though we could, of course, go and visit Him in the Church. He was remote and distant from us in time and place, though always watching, always waiting for us to do something wrong. And then? Brimstone and fire! Slap, slap, slap! Thump, thump, thump!

Then there were the Ten Commandments, also to be learned off by heart. We understood the ones about not killing or stealing or telling lies; they were easy to get your head around. But "thou shalt not covet thy neighbour's wife" was much more complex, as was the very first one: "I am the Lord thy God; thou shalt not have strange Gods before me." At six or seven years of age, this was all rather a lot to take on board!

Sins in those days were divided into two categories, 'Mortal' and 'Venial'. The mortal sins were the worst. So bad, that if you died with one of these on your soul, then you were on that one way street to Hell for all eternity, - no way out and no way back! A mortal sin put a great big black stain on your soul, which was somewhere inside of you, and that great big black stain could only be erased through the Confessional Box, nowhere else. Shakespeare's Lady Macbeth and her inconsolable *"Out, out, damned spot!"* was nothing compared to this!

Venial sins were less serious, and therefore less punishable. They only put a grey or dull white stain on your soul, and could be redeemed by various forms of prayer and penance, such as fasting, plenary indulgences, or denying yourself some of the luxuries of life, - which to us then usually meant giving up sweets for Lent or giving our pennies towards helping the poor children in Africa. A popular indulgence was visiting a grave-yard three times in succession on All Saints' Day or All Souls' Day, but you had to be sure and go right outside the gates of the grave-yard each time and then go back in again; otherwise, it didn't count. Likewise, with your three visits to the Church. You had to go right out and come back in again, and each time say the " Our Father", then repeat the "Hail Mary" three times, and then finish off with the "Glory be to the Father...." And the "Confiteor". That would all result in you acquiring a clean slate. For now! Until the next time! A clean soul! But where exactly was your soul in all of this? That was a difficult one to ascertain! We were never told; and we never found out.

The Confessional was where you got this soul of yours cleansed, by off-loading all your sins, mortal and venial, in not only what you had done, but in your thoughts as well. To with-hold a mortal sin incurred yet another mortal sin on your soul. Then the priest absolved you, and gave you a penance,- prayers you had to say, depending on the frequency and seriousness of your crimes.

The Confessional! What a gloomy, dreaded experience for any child! The stale air in that small box; the darkness; the waiting for the screen to pull across; and all the time trying to remember the list of offences you had so carefully and conscientiously compiled! "Bless me Father, for I have sinned! I have said the Confiteor, Father. Father, it is .........since my last Confession"; followed by the list of your misdeeds.  And then you had to express deep remorse for offending God, and promise you would never do those things again. Despite this, you usually ended up confessing the same each time anyway! And why? Because you had to come up with something each time; you had to confess to some crimes. There was no such thing as not having something to confess. Nobody could be that good! You must have done something wrong! Our repertoire of course, was very limited, compared to what adults would have had to confess! We did not have the same selection to choose from, hence we ended up confessing the same crimes time after time. If you failed to come up with anything, the priest would question and nudge you towards finding something reprimandable. How perverse was that? What was the thinking behind that one? Always guilty of something or other. Always a sinner! We just knew we were bad, and had to be punished. There seemed little point in trying to be good, you got punished anyway! Slap, slap, slap! Thump, thump, thump! It went on and on, day in, day out. Life was supposed to be difficult, full of pain and sorrow, and you just had to struggle on! The odds were all against us though, as this despotic, frightening, punishing God was the one firmly in charge and He saw everything, even your darkest thoughts.

Mother Mary, Our Lady, was softer, kinder, and you could appeal to Her to talk to God on your behalf. You also had your Guardian Angel, who helped you to be good, and who would be very disappointed in you when you failed. There must have been an awful lot of disappointed Guardian Angels around! I remember a girl in my class asking the nun what was a mortal sin. And the answer she got? - Anything you would not like your parents see you doing! Well, that certainly narrowed things down a lot! I thought immediately of how we all picked our noses or went to the loo, - so we must all be pretty bad. Downright evil, more like! Definitely destined to burn in Hell for all eternity.

Religious teachings and doctrine dominated our lives. Religious feast days permeated the Church year. Lent was a time of fast and abstinence, no this, no that, ending with the long and gruelling services of Holy Week. And all in Latin! The priest, with his back to us, performing some sort of mystical ritual; the incense; the theatrical costumes. The pomp! The ceremony! The drama! The mitre! The staff! Shakespeare's Cleopatra on the Nile would have paled into insignificance in comparison, especially at the funeral of a Pope! -

*"The barge she sat in, like a burnished throne / Burned on the water: the poop was beaten gold; / Purple the sails, and so perfumed that / The winds were love-sick with them".*

Yes! The Church was certainly a place of drama! The Mass itself centred round the sermon, the pulpit the focal point. From here, we were admonished, condemned, shamed even. Thump! Thump! Thump! It all climaxed during Lent, with the Missions; a week for men; a week for women; and the final week for children. It was during this time that Thump! Thump! Thump! rose to new heights, taking on a whole new life of its own; that thump, thump, thump on the rails of the pulpit reverberating throughout the church.

And the other weapon used to control us? Shame! We were shamed into contributing to this, to that; into doing this, doing that. And how were we shamed? By public announcements from the pulpit as to how much each and every parishioner contributed to the parish dues; the Mass offerings at funerals; contributions for repairs to parochial properties. Peter's Pence was another due to be paid, towards the upkeep of the Pope in Rome.

And shame was also associated with sex. There were no sex education lessons in those days, certainly not in primary school! Sex was taboo,- don't even go there! When something is shrouded in mystery and taboo like sex was then, of course it just increases the curiosity; our covert investigations and discussions into the matter somehow always brought us back to the stork and the cabbage! It all remained a mystery, a shameful secret. I remember my mother being "Churched" after my little brother was born. She had to kneel at the altar rails after Mass on Sunday and the Priest came out and said some prayers over her. I was told she was "being blessed"; whereas in actual fact she was being "cleansed"; she had defiled her body through sex and child-birth!

The greatest fear of all, though, to my young mind, was the fear of the Last Judgement at the end of the world, when, at the signal from the Angels blowing their trumpets, all bodies in graves throughout the world would rise up and be judged, yet again, for a final time. What about those who were already in Heaven or Hell? Would they have to come out from wherever they were and be re-admitted? Those fortunate enough to be directed towards Heaven yet again, would praise God for all eternity, sitting around on fluffy clouds playing a musical instrument, or singing hymns. For all eternity? How could anyone possibly know that amount of hymns? And would the novelty not wear off after a while? What would we then find to do? And what would happen to those who were still alive on that last day? Would they all just ascend into Heaven, up through the clouds, a bit like Jesus had done? Heaven must be a huge place to accommodate all those numerous people. But then we weren't all destined to go to Heaven anyway!

Yes! The Church controlled every aspect of our lives, with the priest taking on the role of mediator between us and God. Special permission had to be applied for if a woman needed a hysterectomy; bishopric approval and consent was necessary if anyone wanted to go to Trinity College in Dublin; and if a Catholic wanted to marry a Protestant, then the Protestant had to sign an agreement that the children would be brought up in the Catholic Faith. How arrogant was that! Schools were controlled by the clergy; divorce was not tolerated, and if someone did separate from their partner, then that person was denied Holy Communion.

The Church was a rigid, uncompromising, unbending shadow that hung over everything and everybody. It lurked in all corners, even in the car-park after the Sunday night dances!

The God of my childhood was non-existent; an imaginative figment born out of fear and a lust for power and control. Slap, slap, slap! Thump, thump, thump!

# Chapter 2

## That was then; this is now

It was all about Religion in those days, all about being holy, whatever that meant. Nothing about Spirituality.

I now see Religion and Spirituality as being two very different concepts.

Religion is merely a label, a name, a brand, and has been used throughout History as a means to many ends. Religion is a divisive force, not a unifying force. Wars have been fought over religion; entire nations have been divided over religious affiliations; families have been split over religion; murders have been committed too terrible to think about, all in the name of religion. Adherence to a particular religion has unleashed unimaginable extremes in violence. Countries have been conquered and settled in the name of religion. Religion has been used to incite hatred, murder, revenge. Religion has divided men for numbers of reasons. And religion can be instilled into any of us, at any stage of our life, manipulating us, controlling us, intimidating us, depending on the various techniques used. We need to experience opposites though, - pain/joy; sorrow/ happiness, and by being subjected to dictatorial and controlling religious regimes, we search for the truth and liberate ourselves from such regimes as part of our progress towards Ascension.

And how does the concept of Spirituality differ from that of religion?

Spirituality transcends all religions. Spirituality cannot be instilled into us by any external force. Spirituality is our own individual connection to Spirit, and we must all find that connection for ourselves; we cannot inherit that connection from our parents or ancestors - unlike religion. Spirituality is an inner knowing that there is a much greater force than us in control of all aspects of life in the world and in the Universe. Spirituality is not a show, a display, a flamboyance. Spirituality does not seek approval or recognition in outward displays of prayers or religious rituals. And Spirituality is an understanding and an acceptance that we are all of Divine Essence, and we are all one.

Religious institutions are disintegrating, as more and more people realise that their own spiritual needs and requirements are not being fulfilled. People everywhere are searching for a deeper meaning to life. And that cannot be found in controlling religious regimes. Deep peace and fulfilment can only be found through one's own Spiritual connection to Source. Spirituality allows your Soul to fly freely, unfettered and unchained, released from the cage of enclosed thinking, from the confines of absolutism; from the dictates of those who profess to know what is best for you, for your Soul, your own unique Soul; from the control and manipulation of those who claim to have all the answers. Spirituality enables you to find all the answers within yourself, in your own magnificent, inherent Divine Essence, instead of looking to outside influences. The only person who knows what is best for you is you yourself; and when you connect with Divine Source through your own Soul, through your own Spirituality, then you are serving your own highest good.

The place in which I now am, at this point in time, is a place of deep Spirituality: a deep recognition of my own connection to Source; a deep recognition that we are all part of the vast network of Divine Universal Energy; and a deep inherent knowing that we are all on our way back to Source, individually and collectively, from whence we all came. The place where I am now is not affiliated to any one particular religion; where I am now transcends religion; where I am now is a sanctuary from controlling religious beliefs and dogma. My Soul flies freely, as each and every Soul is meant to do. The After-Life now holds no fear for me, unlike in my childhood when I was constantly reminded of the so-called terrors and tortures that await me, and all of us when it comes our turn to "die".

There is a plan for our life, for the earth and for the Universe. Life is a continuous cycle, beginning at birth, ending upon death, and reviewed between lives in the Spiritual Realms. Each new incarnation is undertaken with the sole aim of furthering our Spiritual Ascension, propelled by the soul's innate desire and inclination to progress in wisdom through life-time after life-time, from soul immaturity to full Spiritual Awareness. Each life we undergo has an objective in the learning of the particular lessons we choose to learn each time around, and if we do not learn those lessons in this life-time, we will reincarnate again and again until we do. As advancing souls on the path to full awareness, we have known embodiment many times before on Planet Earth, and we will return for many more life-times. Each of our incarnations is designed to afford us the opportunity to evolve to a higher perspective, both as an individual Soul and as the Collective Soul of all humanity.

We create our own life blue-print; we decide on the lessons we wish to learn; we orchestrate the events and people in our own life drama; we write our own life script, and we review our own progress or lack of it when we pass back again to Spirit. There is no God interfering in any of this. There is no judgement, no condemnation, no punishment. And there is no Hell; there is no Purgatory; there is no Limbo. We have complete free will, always. And there is a reason for absolutely everything that happens to us in our lives, in both the bad times and the good. We are always in the right place at the right time. Our awareness of why we are here will expand when we accept that everything that happens, simply happens; when we accept that every event and person in our lives are all put in place for a purpose; the purpose of our own Soul evolution and the evolution of the Spiritual Consciousness of all humanity.

The laws to which I now adhere are the Seven Spiritual Laws of the Universe. It is adherence to these Spiritual Laws of the Universe that enable us to attain self-mastery, and it is adherence to these same Spiritual Laws of the Universe that enable us to live a life of joy and abundance.

So what are these Spiritual Laws of the Universe, that promise so much, and deliver in their entirety?

Firstly, the Law of Pure Potentiality. The source of all Creation is Pure Consciousness. Pure Consciousness is Pure Potentiality. We are Pure Consciousness, and therefore we are also Pure Potentiality. Pure Potentiality means unlimited, eternal possibility. And we gain access to this pool of eternal possibility through meditation and non-judgement. The qualities inherent in eternal possibility, in Pure Potentiality,- infinite creativity, freedom and bliss,- are freely accessible to us through Nature. We are completely and absolutely unlimited in our state of Pure Consciousness, in what we can achieve and what we can do.

Secondly, the Law of Giving and Receiving. As you give out, so you shall receive. What you give to others comes back to you multiplied many-fold. Also, we need to keep Universal Energy flowing. Like flowing water, energy will become stagnant if blocked. We block the flow of Universal Energy by not keeping a balance between our giving and receiving. Receiving is not the same as taking. Taking implies a one-way movement, not a flow, based on just one person; receiving incorporates involvement of two persons, in a corresponding, synchronised, outward and inward flowing motion.

The Third Spiritual Law of the Universe is the Law of Karma: what you sow, so shall you reap. No exceptions!

Fourthly, The Law of Least Effort. The Universe knows exactly what you need and desire, and re-arranges itself to get all good things to you. By trying to force your own outcome, you are impeding that flow of all good things to you. Not exactly a good idea!

Fifthly, The law of Intent and Desire. You can create what you desire in your life by changing your energy in order to attract like energy to you. Your intention creates your thoughts. And your thoughts, just like your words and actions, go out into the Universal Energy flow and manifest. So!- Be careful what you wish for!

The Sixth Spiritual Law of the Universe? The Law of Detachment. Relinquish your attachment to your desired outcome. The Universe knows the best outcome! Relinquish your attachment to the known, and step into the world of all possibilities.

Finally, The Law of Dharma; The Law of Purpose in Life. We are all here to spread unconditional love; to serve humanity; and to express our own unique talents in helping to raise the Collective Spiritual Consciousness of all humanity. That's it! That is our purpose in life.

These are the laws that guarantee us a life of joy, abundance and fulfilment. But we have never been taught about these laws at any stage in our education. And why have we never been taught about these laws? Because they are Spiritual Laws; they are not the laws of Religion. And remember how I explained the difference in Spirituality and Religion? Spirituality enables our Soul to fly freely; Spirituality enables us to be who we really are, unfettered by the dictates of controlling, manipulating religious dogma, whose laws are promulgated to prevent us from thinking for ourselves. And in This Great Awakening which we are now experiencing, we are seeing the rise of Spirituality and the corresponding fall of Religion. And that can only be good!

And where does God fit into all of this? Who or what exactly is God?

God is not a person. God simply "is". We are collectively God. We are individual pieces of God. In just the same way as the church itself is not any one particular building; the Church is all the members of that institution combined; all the members combined form the Church. So too, God is all of us. We all, together, make up God; we are all combined in God. God is not one, but God is all. All is One; One is all. Absolutely everything that is, ever has been and ever will be, is combined in God. God is not a separate identity; we are all one in God. We are all part of the Divine Energy that runs through and supports all forms of life on our Planet Earth, in the Universe and in the entire Cosmos. We are all held together in the most exquisite, the most elaborate, the most ingenious network of sacred geometry, mathematical equations and Spiritual vibrations. We are all an equal part of the whole, the whole being God in all its entirety.

# Chapter 3

# My Own Metamorphosis

So how did I get from where I was, back then in my primary school days, to where I am now? How and when was this God of my childhood unmasked for me? What were the influences that brought this unmasking about?

There were four factors prompting this unmasking. First, my studying and then teaching of History and English; second, I began to travel; third, my own developing deep affinity with Nature and the Elemental Kingdoms; and last but not least, my introduction to Reiki and the whole vast area of working with Celestial Divine Healing Energies. The synchronistic influences of all these have led me to where I am today; have led me to find the place in the Universe, reserved just for me, in just the same way as there is a place reserved for each and every one of us. When we find that place, we live in joy, abundance and fulfilment, in harmony with all forms of life around us. When we do not try to find that place, we suffer emotionally, spiritually, and ultimately, physically.

My secondary education school days ushered in a whole new wonderful phase of my life, one where slap, slap, slap; thump, thump, thump were gone, gone for good. In my thirst for learning and knowledge, I flourished and revelled in the carrot rather than the stick. My favourite subjects? History and English.

It was through the study of these two subjects that I began to realise that things were not as I had been led to believe in my earlier years. It was through these two subjects that I began to see things differently; it was through these two subjects that I began to question everything

I had ever been taught. And it was through these two subjects that I began to think, - something that had always been denied me in my primary school days.

I had always been an avid reader. My father was always reading, and it was he who introduced me to the works of Charles Dickens and Robert Louis Stevenson when I was still at primary school. He paid me a shilling, a lot of money in those days, for every Dickens' novel I read. And I never cheated! I read every word! I just loved reading about Oliver Twist, Mr. Bumble, Pip, Nicholas Nickleby, Ebenezer Scrooge, the Cratchits, and all the other fascinating characters who peeped out at me from those pages! Those books were an education in themselves, reflections of life as it really was in Dickensian times. Fascinating! The God of those Dickensian and Victorian times though, was still a very austere God; still punishing, still directing souls to Heaven or to Hell. But as I progressed naturally from there, in my secondary education school days, to the works of the Brontes, Jane Austen, Chaucer, Shakespeare, Irish writers, writers from other cultures, this austere image began to change, and a different God began to emerge out of the depths of the mists in which He had been enshrouded during my earlier years.

Through my study of History I learned about the abuses in the medieval Church and how those abuses led to the Reformation: the enormous wealth enjoyed by powerful Church men; the control the Church exerted over men's minds; the decadent, worldly, lavish life-styles of the higher clergy and bishops; the involvement of Popes and Cardinals in wars and scandals; the scheming, the cunning, the manipulation that permeated Church ranks; the remoteness of the Church from the ordinary people; the immense wealth amassed by the monasteries; the vast influence the Church had over all matters political; the privileges enjoyed by the clergy, exempted from trial and sentencing in ordinary courts. All this was embodied, given substance, through the characters of Chaucer, in his famous "Canterbury Tales". The Pardoner, who showed no sense at all of the sacred nature of his work, but spent his time manipulating his congregations, through fear and shame, to buy his forged relics, in exchange for a promise of forgiveness for their sins and, ultimately, Redemption. He was certainly good at his job, the best, in fact:

*"Ne was ther swich another pardoner."*

His tricks and cons were all part of the game:

*"For in his male(luggage) he hadde a pilwe-beer, (pillow-case) /Which that he seyde was Oure Lady Veil: /He seyde he hadde a gobet of the seil (piece of the sail) / That Seint Peter hadde, whan that he wente/ Upon the see, til Jhesu Crist him hente ( until Jesus took him into the boat). / He hadde a crois of latoun (brass cross) ful of stones, /And in a glas he hadde pigges bones. /But with thise relikes, whan that he fond/ A povre person (parson)dwelling upon lond, (in the country)/ Upon a day he gat him moore moneye ( the pardoner earned more money in one day )/ Than that the person gat in monthes tweye; ( than the parson in a year). / And thus, with feyned flaterye and japes( pretended flattery and tricks)/ He made the person and the peple his apes."*

The Monk in Chaucer's Tales is equally reprimandable, equally oblivious to the sacred nature of his calling. He is supposed to be in an enclosed Order, living a life of poverty, celibacy and obedience. But where is he? Out enjoying field sports, wining and dining in the best taverns, living a luxurious life!

 Similarly, the Summoner, whose job it was in the medieval Church to summon people to court who had transgressed the laws of the Church in some way, was ready and willing, for a respectable consideration of money, to let his friends defy the ecclesiastical courts and live in sin. Moreover, he tried to suggest that the discipline of the Church could be despised, because a money payment to the

Archdeacon could settle all troubles.

The power and control of the Medieval Church permeated every aspect and area of life. With the growth of towns and trade, producing a new, wealthy, powerful middle class in society, however, and the development of printing, which spread new ideas to many more people, the Church began to lose its tight grip on people's lives.

It was the Reformation, however, that instigated the split in the Church between Catholic and Protestant, and ushered in centuries of conflict; wars and untold violence perpetrated in the name of Religion and God. Political power shifted from Church to Monarchs. This control again, in turn, shifted from Monarchs to Parliaments as a result of the Great Renaissance. This Great Renaissance was a time of questioning of old beliefs and ideas, and an exploring of new ones. The Church fared badly, as a lot of its teachings were found to be wrong, and it strongly opposed any new ideas, clinging desperately to its own dated teachings in a last defiant attempt to retain control over men's souls.

Yes, my study of History and Literature certainly provided me with an understanding of present times. History shows us how we have got to where we now are; and through Literature, we explore human feelings and emotions, and the vast differing reactions to events and circumstances that affect all our lives. And through Literature, we learn that we are all unique in our own experiences and in the expressing of our feelings and thoughts; there is no one right way, just different ways.

The God of my childhood was further unmasked through my travels. Travelling nourishes the Soul, of that I am certain. We see the World in all its grandeur, beauty and glory; the kaleidoscopic display of colours, the diverse and multi-faceted array of life all blending into the unique tableaux that all form our wonderful, amazing, unique

Planet Earth; the life energy pulsating, throbbing, weaving through mountains, oceans, rivers, deserts, plains, tropical forests; through human life, animal and mineral. Travelling awakens us to all of this. And travelling makes us more liberal in our thinking, our understanding, our acceptance of the beliefs and practices of others, and instils into us the realisation that the world does not revolve around our own little corner of the Universe. Of this too, I am certain.

I have witnessed the effects of the displacement of indigenous peoples throughout the entire world; I have seen first-hand the poverty of countries whose natural wealth and resources have been pillaged and plundered by the Great Powers through greed and in their struggle for dominance; I have felt the desperation and pain in the clash of opposing types of life-style as people attempt to adopt western habits, ideas and mercenary attitudes, at the expense of their own more natural followings; I have sensed the loss and heartbreak of those forced to abandon their lands and livelihoods as a result of conflict, a conflict not of their making. And I have witnessed the extremes of wealth and poverty that continue to plague our world: moving mountains of rubbish through which children wade to salvage what they can sell for just a few pence; street beggars with all forms of debility and deformity; women searching through rubbish bins to retrieve old tins and cans for re-selling, again for just a pittance.

But I have also learned about the deep, profound Spirituality that keeps people connected to each other and connected to Spirit. The deep-rooted respect of Australia's Aboriginal peoples for the land that nourishes and supports us; the deep rooted reverence of New Zealand's Maori for the Spirits that watch over all of us; the simple altars in front of all dwellings in Far Eastern countries; their profound belief in a Spiritual Force, greater than us, whom they acknowledge daily; the Great Angkor Wat Temple in Cambodia and all the other temples dotted throughout the landscape, and the saffron-robed monks who dwell in them; the pains-taking arrangements of flowers and fruit piled high upon the heads of the women of Bali as they make their way daily to the temples to have the food blessed and then taken back home to be shared in a meal with the family; the simple ways of life, close to nature, of the Lake Dwellers of Tonle Sap in Cambodia; the Masai Mara of the vast grasslands of Kenya; the semi-nomads of the Arabian and Syrian deserts; those living in sparse conditions along the banks of the River Nile; the simple daily existence of the villagers in Navala in the remote mountain region of Northern Fiji, willingly sharing their meal of rice and vegetables with travellers; the unsophisticated way of life of the Islanders of the South Pacific; - all of these peoples may not have as much as we have in material possessions, but they are far ahead of us in Spirituality. Through seeing all of this, I am of the firm conviction that human nature is inherently good, kind and loving. We all face the same challenges, and perhaps those of us with less to lose are the ones least burdened by what life throws at us. And those of us further removed in time and place from the materialism that engulfs the Western World are the ones who have the deepest connection to Source and to their own inner Spiritual Essence.

The third factor in my own Great Awakening has been my growing affinity with Nature and the Elemental Kingdoms. Growing up in Ireland in the mid-twentieth century, I was, of course, programmed to believe in the Little Folk, the Banshees, Fairies, and of course, the Leprechauns. I never saw or heard any of these, though there were abundant reports from those who did claim to have experienced such an encounter. But as I grew older, this all took on a much deeper meaning for me. I still do not see or hear from other vibrations or dimensions, but I feel, I sense. There is a harmony and correspondence in every living thing in the entire Universe, including the movement of planets, tides, air currents, animals, humans, rocks, crystals, plants, - everything sings its own song of life, the entire synchronised orchestral symphony generating the rhythm of life to which we all respond and to which we all contribute. A luminous, iridescent, sparkling, grandiose show constantly taking place all around us, twirling, spinning, dancing; mind-boggling in its largesse, in its grandeur, as all in the Cosmos responds to certain harmonies and combinations of notes which are tuned to the same scale:

*"The rhythm of life is a powerful beat./ You can feel it in your fingers, / In the tingle of your feet!"*

The Universe is programmed to adapt to all developing situations; the Universe knows exactly how to transform all energy into the creative force that is necessary to sustain qualitative evolution and growth on Planet Earth, in the Universe, and within the entire Cosmos. The Elemental Kingdoms are key to all of this; they sustain and foster the life forms in Nature that keep the pulse of life, the rhythm of life, in synchronistic harmony.

And how do we connect with them? How do we ever get to witness their splendour and energy? By spending time in quiet places; by listening to the silence as it speaks to us; by seeing the splendour unfold before our very eyes; by communicating in thought with the life energy force that flows through the trees, the flowers, the grass. So go on! Hug your trees! Feel the energy pouring out from them to you. Feel the energy from the Elementals looking after, nourishing, pouring life into each and every blade of grass, every leaf, every flower. See how this pouring of each Elemental energy into each facet of Nature results in the different colours, the different shades that swirl and dance around us in the great Cosmic Performance, in the Great Cosmic Dance, in the Greatest Show on Earth. Watch how the trees bend and sway with the wind, never fighting against it or trying to resist. See how the flowers turn their little faces to the sun, for light, warmth and energy. Nature feeds and nourishes the Soul, and time spent in Nature cannot fail to remind you that there is an ever-present Power watching over everything, and in control of everything. Nature is our greatest and best teacher, even our "Nurse" as Wordsworth called "Her". Mother Nature whispers to us, speaks to us, calls out to us, in each and every moment, just looking for recognition, and when we respond to that call, our lives are flooded with gifts and abundance. There are messages carried to us on the winds; images in the clouds; wisdom in the mountains, trees, forests and rocks. There is music in the patter of the rain; melody and harmony in the swish and murmur of the ebb and flow of the tides; in the gushing of the running streams and rivers; in the booming of the thunder; in the chirping, in the twittering, in the tweeting of the bird song. The full orchestra! In full blast! Most of us, though, sadly, have lost the ability to tune into Mother Nature, due to the development of modern technology and our increasingly pressured life-styles.

The most recent, but by no means the least influence in my own metamorphosis, has been my introduction to Reiki Healing and the whole vast field of Energy: Universal and Divine Energy; the Energy that flows through every form of life in the entire Cosmos. And Reiki is all about working with this Universal and Divine flow of Energy. Everything is Energy. We have always been in existence as some form of Energy, and we always will be in existence as some form of Energy. Just five years ago, during my first sacred attunement to Reiki, I underwent my first ever Spiritual experience, an experience so profound that it has changed my whole life, irrevocably. I had waited a long time for such an experience, but these things come to us all in Divine timing, not at our bidding. As the sacred Reiki symbols were being attuned into my aura, I felt myself surrounded and held by what I can only explain as the strongest sense of complete and total unconditional love, a warm balm of soothing, a cocoon of absolute belonging, from which I did not want to emerge. It was not my imagination; I am not given to flights of fancy. I felt that Energy around me. It was palpable, tangible. And as the tears continued to flow down my face, something inside me was released. I realised, there and then, that I had given my power away; I had given my power away to others who claimed to know all the answers; I had allowed others to dictate to me my connection with Spirit. I knew instinctively, at that one moment in time, when time itself stood still for me, when time no longer existed, that I was experiencing the true meaning of God: Oneness with all other forms of life; Oneness with All That Is; a true sense of belonging. For the first time in my entire life, I felt my Soul. For the first time in my life I understood. For the first time in my life I felt my connection with Spirit. My Soul was released that day; released from the chains that had bound it all my life. That Energy that I felt around me, and holding me, supporting me that day, the Energy to which I was introduced that day for the very first time, is now the Energy which dictates every aspect of my life, all my waking and sleeping hours. Nothing in my life had prepared me for what happened me that day, and nothing, absolutely nothing, has ever impacted on me in any way remotely like the impact that experience has had on me. That was Spirit connecting with me, as Spirit does with all of us at some stage or other. We are all different, and Spirit connects with us all in a different way, when the time is right. We cannot hurry on or force our own Connection with Spirit; it will happen when the time is right, as does everything in our lives. I now try and live my life according to the five Reiki Spiritual principles: Just for today, I shall not worry; just for today, I shall live and work honestly; just for today I shall accept my many blessings; just for today I shall not anger; just for today I shall respect the rights of all other forms of life.

I had always been aware of a presence around me as a child; my guardian Angel, someone or something looking after me, making things happen, making things work out right for me. In my mid-thirties I began to read about Angels. And not just about Angels. I bought and read every book I could find on Spiritual issues; the meaning of life and death; chakras; auras; Spirit Guides; Ascended Masters; the Celestial Kingdoms; the Elementals; Re-incarnation; past-life regression; the Soul; the Higher Self; Near-Death experiences; the After-Life; books written by Psychics, by Spiritual Mediums; Tibetan books on Living and Dying; Atlantis; Lemuria; life in other dimensions. Many times as I read, I felt myself exclaiming "I know this". In other words, I was tapping into my own inner, deep, inherent knowing, into my own Spiritual Being, my Soul, that knows everything, absolutely everything. This is This Great Awakening that we are all experiencing now, in these unique times.

I am now a practitioner and teacher of many types of Universal and Divine Healing Energy. Yes, the Energy is all coming from the same Source, but it is being channelled through varying frequencies or vibrations. Much like a warehouse, where all the goods are stored, and then moved out in different directions, to different shops; but you get the same in the tin of beans you buy at your local supermarket as the person who buys a tin of beans a few hundred miles away in a different supermarket; all the beans are coming from the same source. So it is with Energy Healing. It is all coming from Source. Each has a unique feeling: The Christ Consciousness Energy is very strong, while Mother Mary Energy is milder, softer; Archangel Michael's Energy is stronger, hotter, than the calmer, soothing healing Energy of Archangel Raphael. And yet again, Unicorn energy feels very different from the Energy of the Dolphin, the Dragon, or the Elementals. Yes, the Unicorns, the Dragons are real, and they are here in abundance, invisible to the human eye, of course, as they operate on a much higher vibration, the same high vibration as the Archangels, a vibration of pure Light and Love.

I still do not see or hear Angels, or any other form of Celestial Beings. But I sense them all around; I sense the different Energy that accompanies each one; I sense when a different Energy enters a room; what Energy comes in for a particular healing; what particular Energy comes in to connect with a loved one still here in this incarnation; the Energies in a person's aura. And it is a great privilege for me to be able to teach others how to connect with Spiritual Universal Energy; how to protect themselves from negative or dark Energies; and yes, there are a great deal of lower, dark Energies about. It is also a very beautiful moment when I can help people connect with their loved ones who have passed back to Spirit, and enable them to receive and give a message, whether it is a young child, parents, grand-parents, or siblings. In all of this, I am not the Healer; I am merely the conduit, the channel, the portal, the gateway, through which the Energy flows. Spirit is using me as a pathway to get to others, and the fact that I have now been attuned to so many different forms of Higher Spiritual Energy Healing makes me more susceptible, more sensitive. Each and every one of us is a channel, a portal, through which the infinite love of Spirit reaches others. When the time is right for each of us, that will all be activated, but we all need to be tuned into our own Spiritual nature, in order for it to happen, and in This Great Awakening, occurring right now, we are all experiencing a feeling of some deeper connection with Source and our own Soul and Higher Self.

# PART TWO:

# This Great Awakening

## Chapter 4

## What is This Great Awakening?

Christ Himself said: *"He who has eyes to see, let him see; he who has ears to hear, let him hear."*

Everything changes; absolutely everything is in a constant flux of change; change is the inherent nature of life. And so be it.

We are living in a time of enormous changes, affecting each and every aspect of our lives. There is A Great Awakening taking place all around us, tangible, palpable. Humanity is on the path of Ascension, a process of the raising of spiritual consciousness, as we evolve into a higher vibration species.

So what exactly is This Great Awakening?

This Great Awakening is the process by which we are emerging from our long sleep of forgetfulness into a remembering of who and what we really are. We are now breaking out of our illusion; the illusion that we are all a separate identity, entire and complete in ourselves. We are now awakening to the realisation, the remembering, the accepting, that there is no separateness: no separateness from each and every other of us; no separateness from each and every other form of life; and no separateness from Source.

To understand This Great Awakening process, we first need to understand the cyclical nature of all things. Everything moves in cycles: the earth's orbital motion around the sun, bringing the cycle of the four seasons; cycles of the Moon, bringing the ebb and flow of the tides; the cycle of birth, death and re-birth; even the rise and fall of great civilisations, great dynasties; and of most relevance for us here, the great cycle of forgetting and remembering.

And it is this great cycle of forgetting and remembering that is determining the present process of This Great Awakening. We are awakening from a long forgetting of our true spiritual inherent nature, our Divine origins. We forgot, we lost, our connection to Divine Source over two thousand years ago. And with that forgetting, that dis-connection, came the descent into depravity, gross materialism, the pursuit of the individual ego as opposed to the collective responsibility. Since the fall of Atlantis, in fact, humanity has been on this downward spiral into the lower vibration levels, deviating further and further from Divine Source. We are now faced with the grave situation confronting our Planet Earth regarding the serious lack of respect for one's self, lack of respect for all others, lack of respect for all other forms of life, and lack of respect for Mother Earth herself. Yes, there are many dark energies, many low vibrations amongst us here on Earth: greed; corruption; violence; poverty; drugs; all being fed and given substance and credence by the media and the human lower- based ego.

It is at this time however, that a vast number of enlightened souls are embodied here on Earth, to help in This Great Awakening process, to waken us all up; to waken us all up out of our long period of forgetting, and into this period of remembering who and what we really are.

What is happening to us in This Great Awakening is that Light surges of high voltage Divine Energy are penetrating Earth's energy vibration, containing codes and symbols to decode and unlock what has been embedded in us for aeons and aeons of time. Old memories and wounds, together with more specific memories and information deep within our consciousness, are now all rising to the surface; old entrenched beliefs, distant past life memories are all surfacing, bringing us face to face with our Akashic records, giving us the opportunity to clear those records once and for all, and to ascend into a higher spiritual vibration on our path to Enlightenment. The Akashic records are a spiritual accounts book of all we have been and all we have ever done in our entire existence; everything is recorded in Spirit, and we will have total access to our own personal Akashic records when we pass back to Spirit and review our own life, in order to assess how well we learned the lessons we came here to learn, and whether or not we need to return for another round to try and improve upon our performance. At this time, in This Great Awakening, we are remembering more and more details from our Akashic records, and we are realising that what is happening to us, the people we meet, are all affording us golden opportunities to help clear those Akashic records. All cellular memories must be cleared and purified; if not, then the lessons associated with each memory, the lessons we ourselves freely chose to learn, will keep re-presenting themselves to us until we do.

All of us are wakening up to a realisation that we know, we "just know" certain bits of information; information that we have always known, but which we have long forgotten. We are finding ourselves exclaiming more and more often "Oh! I know that!" Each time you do this, you are remembering another forgotten piece of the jig-saw, you are awakening to the realisation that you yourself have all the answers inside you, to all the questions you could ever ask. You are decoding, piece by piece, bit by bit, that which has lain dormant in you for so long, and is now being re-awakened in you in This Great Awakening.

Enjoy!

# Chapter 5

# Why now?

Why is This Great Awakening happening now?

Let me explain.

John Donne, the Metaphysical poet (1572-1631), in his famous poem "A Valediction Forbidding Mourning", compared his relationship with his wife to the two legs of a compass (his father was a wealthy ironmonger!). A relationship based on sensual attraction is vulnerable to periods of absence, but a relationship based on a love which is not dependent on the physical senses is built on strength and endurance.

Yes, Donne was referring to his relationship with his wife, but if we look closer, we can see that this also applies to our relationship with God, with our Divine Source, a connection that cannot ever be broken. As Donne compares his connection with his wife to the two legs of a compass, so too, we can use the same comparison for our connection to Source. We are, as Donne says, but *"an expansion, / Like gold to ayery thinnesse beate."* In other words, we are of the same substance. We are like the legs of a compass: one leg is rooted firmly, the other expands outwards and travels round, constantly expanding and contracting, but always remaining firmly connected to the grounded leg, its source, and always returning to that source, to that fixed position, without which, the travelling leg of the compass has no meaning. Its very existence is only as a travelling composite of the fixed point. Donne writes:

*"As stiffe twin compasses are two, / Thy soule the fixt foot, makes no show / To move, but doth, if the' other doe. / And though it in the center sit, / Yet when the*

*other far doth rome, / It leanes, and hearkens after it, / And grows erect, as that comes home./ Such wilt thou be to mee, who must / Like th'other foot, obliquely runne; / Thy firmness drawes my circle just, / And makes me end, where I begunne."*

See the comparison? The comparison between our relationship with Divine Source and the two legs of a compass. One leg, Divine Source, is firmly fixed; the other leg is travelling, contracting and retracting, but always returning to the fixed leg, without which it has no meaning, no reason for existence. They both act at all times as one.

What has this comparison all got to do with This Great Awakening we are now experiencing?

We have come from Source, into this and every incarnation, to learn particular lessons; lessons we ourselves have freely chosen to learn. In the process of learning these lessons, and because we always have free will, we can, again and again, freely choose to deviate from our previously chosen path. But we are always connected to our origins, our Divine Source. It is not like an elastic band, which, when stretched too far, will snap and break. We can travel wherever we like, but that connection is unbreakable, indissoluble, infinite. And at the end of each incarnation, we always return to where we began.

At this point in the history of mankind, we are on the contracting movement, the returning back to Source. Mankind, over the last two thousand years, lost its way, circling round and round in the lower vibrations, forgetting its Divine Source connection. We are now on the return journey, after a long absence. We are now remembering what we have always known, but freely chose to forget in our pursuit of earthly pleasures, adopting all the lower based attributes, falling more and more into a sense of self, into self-ishness, forgetting who and what we really are. But, just like in the case of the two legs of the compass, the time comes when we return to Source. And that time is now!

Now is the time! The great surge into earth's vibration of all the higher energy forces began with the Harmonic Convergence in 1987. This was the name given to one of the world's first globally synchronised meditation events, on August 16-17, 1987, which also closely coincided with an exceptional alignment of planets in our Solar System. This great inward surge of higher energy vibrations reached a great peak in 2012, with the never-before re-alignment of the planets, ending both a 26,000 year Cosmic cycle and a 260,000 year Cosmic cycle. Something happened in 2012 that never happened before! And what, exactly, happened in 2012? Earth and all the other planets became as one, their magnetic and spiritual energies merged, raising the denser vibration on earth. What is possible now, for the first time, was not possible a century ago. We are now working with more subtle energies. Divine waves of Light are now flooding our planet as a result of this convergence of the planets in 2012, and lifting us all to the level of Light. And what does light do? It shows up everything; all the darker forces, all the cobwebs, all the dust, all the places that need cleaned! And that is what is happening right now. A great cleansing is under way; a cleansing that is necessary to rid the earth of all that is negative; and then the new can be installed. We are all being awakened to the information encoded in our chakras, especially the higher ones, unconsciously wakening us up to more and more of our true identity. This Divine Wisdom entering our Planet is emerging as higher knowing in people of the Light, as we all decide who we really are; as we discard the former attractions of the lower way of living, as that will no longer be of any interest to us; and as we reclaim our Divine inherent nature. And the speed at which this is all happening is gathering remarkable momentum!

We can see the signs of This Great Awakening all around us. Former great establishments are toppling; governments; financial institutions; economic systems. Everything is coming out into the open, to be seen and reformed or discarded. But not only all that!

Everyone is now questioning, asking, looking for answers as to the reason why we are all here. Young and old alike are raising their heads, looking upwards, searching for the Light; realising that there is more to us all than just this mortal body. That Light is now surging in from above, awakening us all to who and what we really are! God Essence! The codes embedded in us are being decoded. We are awakening! We are reclaiming our power! All is good! All is as it should be!

# Chapter 6

# Why is it different this time?

History is littered with intermittent, recurring periods of religious zeal, all claiming to be a Great Awakening. Zealous reformers, urging congregations to return to an adherence to religious teachings, religious doctrines, religious rituals, have come and gone down through the centuries. All have faded into the mists of time, many having amassed vast fortunes in the manipulation of the human constant search for a deeper and more meaningful connection to all things spiritual. Fire and brimstone, threats of eternal damnation or promises of salvation have all been used by religious fanatics, posing as saviours, promising to lead people back to God. Periods of religious enthusiasm have, time and again, brought a sense of connection and redemption on the part of those affected, and the formation of new religious movements and denominations have all resulted in an increase in religion, but not necessarily in an increase in Spirituality, or even in an understanding of Spirituality.

So what is different about This Great Awakening we are now currently experiencing?

Firstly, all those former so-called Great Awakenings were not Great Awakenings. They were revivals or reformations, not Awakenings. They were fuelled by external forces, an outer stimulus, using the manipulative tools of fear and shame, and of course, money! A typical example of one of these so-called Great Awakenings was George Whitefield, a Minister from Britain, who toured the American colonies in an attempt at proselytising the natives. An actor by training, he certainly knew how to put on a great show. Weeping with sorrow, trembling with passion, he roared and thundered out the Word of God, delivering his sermons to the thousands who flocked to him. He converted slaves and even some Native Americans. And he made money in the process! How can that be called a Great Awakening?

Secondly, the only other event in History that can be regarded as an Awakening was the great Renaissance of the Middle Ages. And why? Because it awakened man's curiosity in the outside world, leading him to investigate, to explore, to question, to no longer accept the teachings of the old Masters, but to go and investigate for themselves. And in investigating for themselves, they discovered that a lot of what the old Masters had taught was wrong. The world was not flat; you did not fall over the edge, and there were no monsters of the deep. Neither did the sun revolve around the earth. The Renaissance ushered in a period of investigation for oneself, seeing things exactly as they were instead of what they were just thought to be. This new age of inquiring, investigating, exploring, was dominated by men like Michael Angelo, Christopher Columbus, Francis Drake, Copernicus, Galileo, - all of whom awakened men's curiosity and interest in the world in which they lived. But again, this was an Awakening to the outside world, the physical world, in a response to outer stimuli.

Thirdly, this present Great Awakening is different in both its nature and the circumstances surrounding it. It is not fuelled by external physical forces. This is an inward looking movement, an Awakening on the part of each individual, to an awareness, a remembering, of our own inherent Divine nature, our own infinite connection with Source and with All That Is. It is not driven by religious fanaticism or controlling sects; but instead by an inherent knowing within each of us that we are of Divine Origin, and we are now, of our own free will, reclaiming that Divine Origin.

Finally, the 2012 unique convergence of the planets in our Solar System has given this Great Awakening the energy, the power, the vibrational lift to enable us to Awaken to what we were not able to see before. The great in-surge of Celestial Light that is currently flooding our planet as a result of what happened in 2012 has brought us a massive shift in spirituality as opposed to religion, freeing us from the chains which had kept us in bondage for centuries and centuries, allowing our souls to fly freely, without fear, for the first time since the fall of Atlantis.

So, this time it is different. Never before has there been anything like what is happening on Planet Earth at this point in time. We have all chosen to be here now, to help in this Great Awakening. The stage is set, as never before; the circumstances are massively favourable and supportive, as never before; we are awakening spiritually, as never before. Let the show begin! Wakey, wakey! Rise and shine! Our long slumber is over, our time of forgetting has ended. We are now remembering what we have always known. We are experiencing the first Great Spiritual Awakening in the history of humanity. We are on our way back to Source; we are on our way home! And what is there not to like about that?

# Message channelled through Archangel Michael for Fire Spirit Healing Energy (The Christ Consciousness and the Holy Spirit)

## (Translated from the original Spanish)

*"I share this message with affection for all the Beings of Light.*

*Let us allow the love of God to flow, wakening us up as human angels. It is so beautiful to see how human beings waken up in the name and the love of God. We have to make this love flow to our brothers and sisters. We have to do this work; we have to waken ourselves up first and look at ourselves in the mirror, and recognise ourselves and say, "I am a human angel of God because I am a warrior of His Light, and through me, my brothers and sisters can be sure of the existence of God, and of His assistance."*

*It is a beautiful task that we have to do; it is love that we have to waken up in other human angels, and we should tell them with love, that they are a Divine instrument through which flows the love of God. Tell people that they are human angels in their role of being like a mother, when with a gesture, a word, a caress, an attitude, they give us light in our dark moments.*

*They are human angels also when they struggle to fulfil their dream and when they are constantly focused on their spiritual growth. They are human angels too, when they help others to understand that love is the most beautiful thing and that in every way, shape or form, this love is reflecting the infinite love of God.*

*I ask them, "Don't you think it is important for God that you waken up as a human angel and that you waken everyone else up?"*

*For all the Light Workers: Sons and daughters, you know who are the Light Warriors. In this moment, you are incorporating so many changes: economic crisis; job changes; fears; insecurities and many other demons. You can only resist and integrate this process if you live with and for the Light and you can avoid reacting to all the attacks you receive all around in the same way as you can avoid falling into the trap of the black energy of anger.*

*After today, you have to carry the Light to all aspects of your life, integrating two key words: Faith and Humility, and you will win. Only this attitude will open the door of the Heavens, so that you open also the door of the Earth.*

*God gives to you if you are true to yourself. If disparity exists between what you think and feel, and your way of living, you will divide yourself and you will enter into crisis; you will make yourself ill. You will not be receiving the life that you know you deserve, because there will be a blockage in your aura, therefore entering into your energetic field, causing pain, fear, anxiety, chaos, sorrow. Sometimes you will not realise that you have these, but you will, on occasions, physically know, as your physical body could become sick*

*Be aware that if your psychological and emotional bodies don't rise in vibration, you will be exposed to exterior chaos. If there are crevices, then the simple task of getting on the metro, being at work, with people who are anxious, or if there are problems in your home, you will really suffer. Therefore it is essential to raise your vibration.*

*Try to keep a clean energy. It will help to call me when you get up in the morning or when you go to bed at night, or when you get into the car, or at any moment when you perceive danger, or when you feel that something is not right.*

*Another important way to seal yourself is with the prayer the Our Father. Because of His metaphysical significance, He will bring you protection and balance and will open the doors of Heaven and Earth for you, in order to reconnect you with us.*

*Try to do good works in your surroundings. It will help you feel better, to see that goodness is looking after your people, with little gestures, listening to them, with some words and with love.*

*Try to put out some seed from your heart, and the Cosmos will reward you with new opportunities so that you evolve and help our Planet to rise up.*

*Each person will know how to amplify the Light to encourage others. Don't despair, you are doing it right. You will have improved, although sometimes you push too much to the limit, sometimes you can be too stubborn, too dependent on appearances, your environment, and what others might think.*

*It is time to change!*

*We will need help and we will support those who are brave. Therefore, take this leap of faith and you will see how faith in yourselves will open the doors that are made for you, the doors that have been designed for you to realise your purpose in life and your mission. It should be easy, all easy.*

*Remember another thing. Open your eyes and be attentive, because we use lots of signs when you cannot see the path. Open your eyes, children; if not, you will not be able to see either the signs or the path and you will get lost in a well of darkness, which is sometimes so deep that not even we could get you out, if you don't ask us, because of your free will.*

*On certain occasions, we are sad because we lose our Light Warriors, because you are switched off and we suffer because we are aware that the darkness has won the battle. Sometimes we manage to regain those Beings of Light (Warriors) but usually they are fractured, desperate and almost without faith.*

*Be aware that sometimes being fractured takes us to this point, and having chinks in your aura would take you to this point, therefore it is essential to keep your physical, psychological and emotional bodies as clean as possible.*

*We can lose battles, but we must try to avoid losing the war, which we will win with love and faith.*

*Be happy and live faithful to your Soul."*

# PART THREE:

# AWAKENING TO WHO YOU REALLY ARE!

## Chapter 7

## Remember Who You Really Are!

You are not just your physical body and your human personality that accompanies that body. So who actually are you? You are Divine Essence! You are a magnificent, wonderful spiritual being, and as such, you are complete, whole and perfect in every way. At your very core, you are, and always have been, a manifestation of the purest, highest energy. You are a living, incarnate soul, incarnated yet again, with Divine Intelligence and Divine Intent.

And why have you come back yet again, into a physical body?

You have re-incarnated many, many times before, and you will do so, many, many times again, in order to advance and progress as a soul. Each of your incarnations, each of your physical embodiments, has been directed solely at, and centred entirely on, your soul evolution and the collective spiritual advancement of all humanity. The advancement of your soul is your sole(!) reason for being here, and everything that occurs in your life  and every person you connect with, is here for that purpose, - to advance your soul. That's it! End of!

All the knowledge that you accumulate through each of your life-times, all the learning, all the experiences you go through, all the trials and tribulations, benefit and advance not only you as an individual soul, but also the whole of humanity and the entire Universe.

You are here on Planet Earth to progress along the path towards total awareness. And what is total awareness? Total awareness means total acceptance and total understanding that you are Divine Consciousness, temporarily using a physical framework, and all that that acceptance and understanding entails: there is no separation between you and the Divine; there is no separation between the material and the spiritual; and there is no separation between the various forms of life. We are all one; we and God are integrated, all merged into total oneness, into All That Is. Souls are at many different levels of awareness, and no-one else can increase your awareness for you. Only you yourself can do that.

That is your purpose for being here on earth,- to become fully in harmony and sync with all life, to be completely open as a channel of Spirit, as well as a part of Spirit, which animates everything that is, ever has been and ever will be. As your soul advances in awareness, you will increase your own inner knowing, in Divine timing, raising your soul awareness even further, to a total acceptance of the Oneness with all life. And this total acceptance of the Oneness with all life includes complete tolerance of all others, how and what they are; non-judgement; total respect for the free will of all others; total acceptance of your eternal continuity as a spiritual being, and all others; and most important of all, total acceptance that you are a part of God, as is every form and part of life, all equal to each other part.

Once your soul has achieved this level of awareness of total merging with All That Is, life on Planet Earth has nothing more to offer you in the way of learning, unless, of course, you freely choose to reincarnate yet again in order to help others.

Recognising and accepting that you are merged with the Divine, and that, as a spirit, you are of the Divine, is not spiritual arrogance or getting above yourself or your station in life. Far from it! Accepting your Divine Essence is simply you recognising the Divine Spirit within yourself, your own spiritual magnificence, the manifestation of Divine Essence, Divine embodiment.

You are actually four energies merged into one: fire energy; air energy; water energy; and earth energy. Fire energy is your soul energy, entering through your crown chakra, your spirit opening, your link to the Divine and serving to direct your life. The air energy manages your thought process, your cognitive ability, through your mid-brain, creating thought and allowing decision-making about your behaviour. The water energy governs your emotions, your heart chakra, allowing the energy to flow. The earth energy governs your base chakra, your "grounding" chakra, holding you firmly in Mother Earth, through the soles of your feet. Your physical body is just the temporary vehicle to transport all of who you really are through this life-time.

## AFFIRMATIONS ON YOUR OWN BEAUTIFUL "I AM PRESENCE"

- *I Am of Divine origin*

- *I Am Divine Essence*

- *I Am the Divine Made Manifest*

- *I Am Eternal Love*

- *I Am Unconditional Love*

- *I Am Divine Creation*

- *I Am Divine Light in Human Form*

- *I Am Perfect Design*

- *I Am Divine Truth*

- *I Am Divine Breath*

- *I Am Divine Will*

- *I Am Divine Wisdom*

- *I Am One with Source*

- *I Am Peace*

- *I Am abundance*

- *I Am magnificent in my Divine Power*

- *I Am holding inside of me, in my own Spiritual Essence, all the answers to all the questions I could ever ask*

- *I Am One with All Creation*

- *I Am the Beauty God Desires*

- *I Am, I Am, All That I Am*

# Chapter 8

# Your Soul and Your Higher Self

What is the difference between your Soul and your Higher Self?

Your Soul is that over-riding totality of who you are, who and what you have ever been, and who or what you ever will be. Your Soul, not your consciousness, or your ego, is the very essence of who you really are, so it governs every aspect of your living and dying. Your soul encompasses your personality, your fears, your love. It is what is indestructible about you, as it can never be destroyed. The strength of your Soul is not a physical phenomenon; instead it is pure energy, pulsating and radiating throughout your physical body.

Your Soul is attached to your physical body through an energetic connection, referred to as the silver cord. This silver cord is linked to each of your seven major chakras, and is the life-line through which your Soul feeds energy and information into your physical body, just as the umbilical cord attaches the baby in the womb to the mother. When the time comes to pass over back to Spirit, the silver cord stretches, and when it disconnects, that is the point of no return. You are on your way home!

When you re-incarnate into each new life-time, you do not take all of your soul with you; only that part which is sufficient for each earthly journey. The rest of your Soul, the greater part, remains with Spirit. This is your Higher Self. So your Soul is, if you like, only a miniscule part of your Higher Self; your Higher Self being the core of your Soul; and that miniscule part of your soul being the only part you take with you into each life, depending on your particular requirements each time. Your Soul feels trapped inside the confines of your physical body; during hours of sleep, however, that miniscule part of your Soul leaves your body and astral travels, to join its greater part. Sometimes, you waken up with a sharp jerk, from your sleep. That is your soul returning to your physical body, rather hastily, as it sensed you were about to sense it had left!

Your Soul and your Higher Self are merged within your physical body; your Soul being the Higher Self, yes, but with suppressed memories; while the Higher Self is the original, purest form of you. Both are the same, both are merged, except that the Soul is aware of the here and now, with limited memory, whereas your Higher Self knows everything, with no limitations whatsoever.

And why has your Soul got only limited memory?

Your Soul has got only limited memory because again, what is embedded and encoded in your Soul, in that limited memory span, is all you need to know for this life-time. Your Higher Self contains buried sacred information for your total Enlightenment, from all your past life-times, and all your karmic deeds. If your Higher Self were to relate, to disclose this information to your conscious Soul, this would impact on your present life in a way that would be contra-productive for your learning the lessons you have come here to learn. You would, in other words, know too much about yourself for your own present good. You would impede your own progress or soul development. The veil of amnesia has been pulled down over our eyes at birth for a reason! We are not meant or supposed to know everything, - otherwise the whole blue-print for our life, that we so carefully created, would just fall apart!

However, we do have access to our Higher Self, at all times. That's the good news! And the other good news? The other good news is that we have only limited access, for our own soul protection, and only in so far as our Spirit Guides and Angels allow us access.

And how do we access our Higher Self?

We access our Higher Self by "going within".

You "go within" in moments of silence and quiet, away from the hustle and bustle, the noise and turbulence of modern, every-day living. You access your Higher Self through meditation; through the quiet, peace and serenity of the Nature Kingdoms; the tranquillity of quiet reflection; the silence. Just sitting quietly with yourself, acknowledging that you are a spark of the Divine, a spiritual being of the highest vibration, surrounded by Divine White Light and asking that part of you, your Higher Self, that part of you that knows all things, what that part of you would do in that particular situation. Call it your gut instinct, your intuition, whatever; the answer you get back is coming from your Higher Divine Consciousness. Trust! Go with it! Follow your instincts. And why? Because they are Divinely guided! That's why!

Yes! Your own Higher Self, that magnificent, beautiful, spiritual part of you, has all the answers to all the questions you could ever ask!

That's how powerful you really are! The deepest source of wisdom available to any human being is their own magnificent "within", their own magnificent, shining spiritual light, within which are all the answers. That is you yourself tuning in to the limitless, unfathomable source of your own wisdom and knowledge, of your own Higher Self. You yourself are the power that created everything in your life, through your own pre-birth life-plan, and you will continue to do so. By "going within", you release yourself from the role decreed to you by others.

So remember who and what you really are! A beautiful, wonderful, powerful, magnificent being, a Spark of Divine Essence, with all the answers inside yourself, in your own inner knowing, to all the questions you could ever ask. You don't need anyone else to give you any answers, you have them all, deep within yourself, in your own, inherent Spiritual Essence. People need to get away from giving their power to those who profess and claim to know the way to truth, declaring their way to be the only way. If all people were to follow their own individual truths, with respect for each other's truths, then we would have Heaven on earth. That's the way to true Enlightenment; to be who you truly are!  At the level of your Soul, you are perfect and complete, and the purpose of your Soul's life-time is to awaken you to your own goodness and the goodness of all others.

Take back your power! You are the power!  And as a Soul, that power is unlimited! Like many others, you too are now tuning in to your own all-knowing Higher Self, with the realisation, time and time again, "Oh! I know that!" Clear evidence that you are tapping into your own Higher Self. Well done! Soul progress indeed! Enjoy! Enjoy! Enjoy! And know that you deserve only the best!

 Your Spiritual nature is always still right there within, because it is who you really are!

## Meditation:  Meeting Your Higher Self

Each time you re-incarnate, you take only a miniscule portion of your over-all Soul with you, just what you need for your survival this time around. The greater part of your Soul remains with Spirit. This is your Higher Self, the Divine Essence part of you that knows all the answers to all the questions you could ever ask.

## HOW TO CONNECT WITH THAT PART OF YOU THAT IS YOUR HIGHER SELF AND HOW TO FEEL YOUR HIGHER SELF AS YOU:

- *Sit with your back straight, so that your energy can flow more easily up and down your spine*

- *Relax your entire body, starting with your toes, moving up through your feet, legs, thighs, abdomen, lower back, arms, shoulders, neck, jaws, face, head and eyes*

- *Breathe deeply, straightening further your spine, and lifting your chest*

- *Open your Heart Centre. You are now ready to meet your Higher Self. Imagine that you are being joined by many High Beings of Light who are sitting in a circle around you. These Beings are here to assist you in meeting your Higher Self*

- *See a beautiful, radiant, shimmering, shining light beginning to come towards you. This is your Higher Self. Greet and welcome your Higher Self and invite it to come closer. Ask your Higher Self to assist you in making a stronger connection. Feel the love of your Higher Self surrounding you and embracing you*

- *Feel the strong rays of Light coming to you from your Higher Self. Feel your vibration increase as the light touches you. Your Higher Self is now merging and becoming one with you. Feel your molecules and atoms merging with it, as if you are reclaiming a part of your energy.*

- *Let your Higher Self merge with you even more, until all the energy patterns are taking on the radiance of your Higher Self. You and your Higher Self are now one*

- *As your Higher Self, open your breathing to create a greater flow of energy in your body. Straighten your position so that you are sitting as your Higher Self, with confidence and wisdom. Mentally reach as high as you can*

- *Think of a situation about which you want guidance. Ask your Higher Self to give you advice about this situation. Imagine you are a wise teacher and consultant. What advice would you give to yourself on this situation?*

- *As your Higher Self, do you have any other messages? Anything about your Spiritual growth? Your Higher Purpose? Anything else?*

- *Thank your Higher self for becoming one with you and sit as long as you wish as your Higher Self*

- *Know that you can access your Higher Self at any time, but remember that you will have access to your Higher Self only in so far as your guides and angels allow, for your own Spiritual good.*

# Chapter 9

# Which Soul Type Are You?

So, now that you have accepted your own Soul's eternal magnificence, greatness and uniqueness, and the infinite power of you in your own Higher Self, let's delve further into the various Soul types, and see more of who you really are!

There are seven Chakras; there are seven colours of the rainbow; there are seven spiritual energy Rays, which vibrate at different frequencies; there are seven Spiritual Laws of the Universe; and yes! There are seven main Soul archetypes! Which type are you?

There is no hierarchy in the seven different types of Soul Essence, all roles are equal; they are simply just seven different ways for your Soul to be; seven different ways of expressing our own inherent Spiritual Nature in each incarnation that we undertake. We each select, in our own pre-life Soul blue-print, a different type of personality for each life; but we can have many lives as each type, depending on how well we learn the lessons we set out to learn in the guise of that particular body, that particular framework. The special abilities, interests and passions we possess are reflected in that particular Soul Essence we choose to adopt.

So what are these seven main Soul types?

These seven main Soul types, in no particular order of importance, and in broadly speaking terms, as each type has several other spin-offs in each category, are: King; Priest; Scholar; Artisan; Warrior; Server; Sage.

Each of these roles has both a negative manifestation and a positive manifestation. If we live our life in the positive polarity, then we will have a life of true fulfilment of self and true intimacy with others. In that positive playing out of our selected role, we are fulfilling our life's blue-print. However,- remember,- we always have free will, and as humans, we often deviate from that blue-print and go our own way. That is when we adopt the negative role of our particular selected Soul type. And in adopting the negative role, our life is filled with emptiness, frustration and alienation. There is no perfect life. Everyone has difficult obstacles in their path; we are here to learn and we ourselves have chosen those obstacles, so, – bring it on! As a human, you might not understand the bigger picture; but as a soul, you know the reasons why you are here; you know the reasons why you go through issues, even trauma, in your life; and you know the reasons why you have selected your own particular soul type. Each time you re-embark upon a new incarnation, it is "Lights! Camera! Action!" yet again, as you make another entry; play another part; put on another mask; receive another encore.

In the Soul type of the King, we also have politicians, leaders, executives, managers. The positive role in this type is one of absolute responsibility, the characteristics being: masterful; authoritative; commanding; self-assured; decisive; unafraid to change the rules; ability to urge change and to understand criticism. The deviation into the negative manifests in tyranny and dictatorship. And the qualities here? - Harsh; autocratic; imperious; authoritarian; inability to deal with criticism; stubborn; pig-headed. So, are you the King or Leader type? Are you on your positive path, or on the negative path?

The category of the Priest Soul type also includes teachers; healers; humanists; clergy; philanthropists. The positive aspects of this Soul type include: inspiring others to change for the better; empowering; motivating; uplifting; showing fervent vision; bringing out the best in everyone; earnest; enthusiastic. The deviation into the negative in this category leads to fanaticism and controlling religious doctrine. And the qualities here? Fanatical; stern approval; limited vision; dogmatic. So, are you a Priest type of Soul? Are you on your positive path, or on the negative path?

The Scholar type includes those who are naturally curious, studious, academic, analytical ,- abstract thinkers and philosophers; historians; economists; astrologists. The positive aspect of this type brings knowledge and learning from life. And the qualities? Curious; analytical; knowledgeable. The negative path leads to getting lost in theory and abstractions. Qualities here? Aloof; pedantic; observing rather than participating; detached. Are you a Scholar type? Are you on your positive path, or on the negative path?

The Artisan type are the artisans; actors; inventors; engineers; poets; writers; mediators; carpenters; gardeners; anyone who creates. In their positive role, they create and bring good ideas to life. Their qualities include: creative; inventive; imaginative; innovative; sensitive; dexterous. In the negative role, though, they can use their ideas and creativity to manipulate and deceive. In this case, they are fanciful; spaced-out; eccentric; idiosyncratic; inventing striking images to hide behind, for example, hairstyles, clothing, accent, mannerisms. An example of an Artisan taking the negative path was, of course, Hitler. He started out as an impoverished artist, living in Vienna. On the negative path that he freely chose, he still "created" something,- a strong, masterful Germany, a pure race. But at what cost? The untold misery and suffering of millions of people. And of course, all the bad karma he, and the entire German nation along with him, collected. Another example of an Artisan adopting the negative role is those who graffiti or use their creative ability to destroy or incite, as opposed to those who use their creative ability to inspire. And yet another example? Using nuclear power to make weapons of mass destruction rather than harnessing it to help people. Are you an Artisan type of Soul? Are you on your positive path, or on the negative path?

The Warrior type of Soul includes all those who stand up for their own rights and act as the voice for others in their search for their rights; do-good campaigners; fighters for justice, fairness, equality; those who speak out against abuse, intolerance, violation of rights. In their positive role, they influence and encourage others, fighting their battles with them, with a "let's do this!" attitude. They are loyal; masterful; determined; forceful; steadfast; persevering. In their negative role they are assertive; vicious; combative; feisty; bogged down in strategy and logistics. Are you the Warrior type? Are you on your positive path, or on the negative path?

The Server type of Soul includes nurses, doctors, carers, therapists, psychologists, - all those devoted to serving the needs of others. In their positive role, they serve the common good (service). Here they are accommodating; generous; modest; caring; dedicated; unassuming; homely; devoted; altruistic. On the negative side, though, they suffer loss of their own power; they lose sight of themselves, their own needs; they become "servile", in "servitude", rather than in the "service" of the positive role; downtrodden; taken advantage of; used as the proverbial "doormat". Are you the Server type? Are you on your positive path, or on the negative path?

The Sage type of Soul, in the positive role, is delivering spiritual messages, guiding people, communicating. In this positive role, they are endearing; articulate; entertaining; charming; expressive; witty; charismatic; eloquent; gregarious; mischievous. In their negative role, they get stuck on transmission; verbose; effusive; loud; attention-seeking; flamboyant. Are you the Sage type? Are you on your positive path, or on the negative path?

So, what type are you? And are you acting out the positive side of your Soul type, or are you on the negative path?

You have more than likely found that you identify with more than just one of these roles. We are all specialists in whatever type we have chosen. Priests and Servers both fit into the category of inspirational specialists: bringing good intentions to life, serving a good cause, seeking to improve the quality of life for all. Sages and Artisans both are expressive specialists: bringing good ideas to life, giving form or voice to thoughts and feelings, changing perspectives. Kings and Warriors both are action specialists: bringing concrete objectives to life, making things happen, setting goals and moving towards them. The Scholar is an assimilation specialist, playing a neutral role, while absorbing knowledge from life.

So, you are most likely identifying with two or even more of these seven Soul types. Our Soul type is often more evident in the early stages of life, when we are still closely connected to Source, and our vibrations are higher than those of adults. As we grow older, however, we lose the connection to Source, as we become attuned to this world and its cultural programming. We adopt a superficial identity, a worldly mask, which has nothing to do with who we really are. It is not until about mid-life or after (mid-life crisis!) that we manage to break through this mask and return once again to a searching for our true identity. Before this stage, we are caught up in life, finding our career, paying a mortgage, raising a family, living in the physical world. It is completely natural for people, as they grow older, to seek out more meaning to life, while the younger are fulfilling their basic needs, and, indeed, pursuing pleasure. While our Soul type permanently stays the same, everything else can change, from one incarnation to another, - religion, race, gender, body shape, etc., but the essence and consciousness of our Soul will be consistent.

# Chapter 10

# The Seven Spiritual Energy Rays

Our Soul is also influenced by the Seven Spiritual Energy Rays, as each soul, as well as each spirit guide, is imbued with at least two of these Seven Energy Rays.

The Seven Spiritual Energy Rays are a mystical belief structure, in existence since at least 600 B.C., that partitions Divine Force into seven energies of equal importance. Each Soul has a combination of at least two of these rays, which dictates their life path, and which can come in at any stage of their life, and not necessarily just at the beginning.

A Ray is a vibrational energy, part of the Christ Consciousness. The energy of these seven Rays, when used on the earth's plane, is the responsibility of a higher Spiritual Being, called an 'Ascended Master', or Cohan. The best known of the Rays is probably The Violet Ray, the Violet Flame. Each Ray reflects a different aspect of the Divine: Ray 1: the Will of God; Ray 2: the Wisdom of god; Ray 3: the love of God; Ray 4: the Purity of God; Ray 5: the Science of God; Ray 6: the Peace of God; and Ray 7: the Freedom of God.

The Universe has been Divinely programmed, and therefore knows exactly how to transform all energy into the creative force that is necessary to sustain evolution and positive growth on Planet Earth, and, of course, within this part of the Galaxy. So let's look more closely at these seven Spiritual Energy Rays.

Life Force simply is. It is a neutral, undirected energy that surrounds and supports the vitality of all beings. Spiritual Energy, on the other hand, has a spiritual quality. It is energy infused with a Force greater than our own, a Divine Intention. This is also the organising force behind all the synchronicities flooding our lives when we open ourselves to our Divine Spiritual Connection.

Ray One of the Seven Spiritual Energy Rays, the Will of God, is the responsibility of the Ascended Master, El Morya. This ray opens lightworkers' throat chakras to speak the truth, and brings faith, protection and power, influencing the King and Leader type of Soul, to carry out God's will and purpose.

Ray Two operates on the crown chakra, under the direction of the Ascended Master Lord Lanto, bringing wisdom and understanding. This ray influences the Priest type of Soul.

Ray Three, is under the direction of Ascended Master, Paul the Venetian, and works on the heart chakra, bringing love, compassion and charity. This ray influences the Scholar type of Soul, as they adapt the universal mind or consciousness to the lifestyle and morality of every-day human existence.

Ray Four is under Serapis Bey, and works on the base chakra, bringing purity and holiness; harmony through conflict; trust; hope; joy and excellence. This ray influences the Artisan type of soul, creating balance and harmony; a merging of elements, like an Artisan.

Ray Five works on the Third Eye chakra, under Hilarion, and brings wholeness and abundance, concrete knowledge and Science. This ray influences the Warrior type of Soul, helping to implement knowledge of how to make things happen.

Ray Six is under Lady Nada, and works on the Solar Plexus. This ray influences the Server type of Soul, bringing peace, service and brotherhood, with idealism and devotion.

Ray Seven is linked to the Violet Flame, under Saint Germaine, bringing ceremonial order, alchemy, justice, mercy, Soul freedom, transmutation and healing, influencing the Sage soul type, in their work of merging the elements for transformation, and teaching spiritual knowledge that we are eternal consciousness.

So, as we can see, our Soul type is not left to random in any way. Rather, there is an over-riding management of souls and consciousness. Each Soul also belongs to its 'Soul Monad', its spiritual family. And there are twelve souls in each Monad. It is to your own individual Monad that your Soul gravitates automatically, when it crosses back to Spirit as you exit this incarnation. Your Monad may include members of your earth family, but not necessarily so.

So, remember who you really are! You are an amazing, inter-dimensional, eternal Cosmic traveller; explorer; adventurer. You always have been, and you always will be, on your long walk-about across infinity, with this life-time being only one miniscule phase of that eternal walk-about. You have bravely and courageously volunteered to come to Planet Earth, yet again, undertaking an intense course of spiritual training, serving two masters: your own soul development; and the collective spiritual awareness of all humanity. You are the bringer of pure Divine Love and understanding; the bringer of spiritual knowledge and Divine connection; the bringer of the realisation that we are all Divinely connected; the bringer of the understanding that God is not one, God is all; and the bringer of the knowledge that we are united in the great All That Is. You are the portal for Divine love and unity to reach all humanity. And as such, you are indeed awesome in your greatness, in your power, as you reach out to collective humanity, raising collective spiritual consciousness and the vibration of the entire Universe.

# Meditation Exercise:   Opening the Third Eye

- *Relax, either in a comfortable sitting or lying position*

- *Ground and protect yourself*

- *Visualise a beautiful garden with a river running through it*

- *Put one hand in the river; in the other hand, carry an amethyst*

- *Close your eyes, focusing your attention upwards towards the centre of your forehead*

- *Concentrate on your Third Eye. See it as closed*

- *Now see this Eye slowly opening. Keep trying!*

- *When you can picture the Eye opened, look into it, into the depths of your own Soul*

- *See the Universe, the Galaxy, all of Space in the depths of your Eye*

- *See the Past, the Present, the Future, all rolled into one, no beginning, no ending, just the vast space of infinity*

- *See a figure coming towards you; Christ. Spend time soaking up the Energy.*

- *Thank the Christ Consciousness for being with you*

- *Come back to the river. Take your hand out of the water.*

- *Concentrate on your Third Eye again, this time closing it.*

- *Keep practising!*

# Meditation Exercise: Raising your Vibration

The purpose of this exercise is to open your heart centre and use your awakened heart to open and balance your energies at many levels, from the physical to the spiritual.

- *Sit or lie down comfortably*

- *Ground and protect yourself*

- *Place your hand over your heart and say with feeling: "I love you; I accept you exactly as you are. I commit to you. I am important. My life counts. I am a magnificent being, a manifestation of the Divine."*

- *Repeat until you can feel the truth*

- *Ask your heart to guide you to follow its loving way. Ask it to speak to you more clearly. Tell your heart you will listen. You can trust your heart, for it will always lead you to your highest good. Put your hand down again gently*

- *Imagine your heart as a star, and let it radiate Love and Light to every cell in your entire body. Feel the Light from your heart balancing, harmonising, re-energising and re-generating your body, enhancing the flow of life-force energy throughout*

- *Ask that your heart be pure and your energy strong and without fear, and with love and respect for all*

- *Accept any emotions that present themselves right now. Send love to each as you identify them*

- *Listen to your thoughts as they come into your mind. Send love to each thought as it registers*

- *When you are ready, open your eyes, take a deep breath and feel the glow of love throughout your body*

Eileen McCourt

# PART FOUR:

# AWAKENING TO THE TRUE UNDERSTANDING OF THE TEACHINGS OF CHRIST

## Chapter 11

## Love One Another

Let me remind you of the one commandment we have been given: Love one another!

But what exactly does this mean? How do we love one another? Coming over all amorous, lovey-dovey, Valentine cards? Hardly!

Very often, an explanation or a meaning is so overt, so obvious, that we fail to see it.

"Love one Another" has a very simple and obvious explanation. It simply means, seeing, first of all, yourself, as the pure Divine Essence you really are, and then recognising that same pure Divine Essence in each and every other person with whom you come into contact. It means looking beyond the physical body, looking beyond the physical imperfections, looking beyond the physical flaws and weaknesses, to the pure, perfect Spiritual Beings we all are, a spark of the Divine, and as such, we can do no wrong; we are perfect in every way.

Let me ask you a question! If Christ or any other Celestial Being were to manifest in front of you right now, what would you do? How would you react? How would you treat that Celestial Being? Apart, of course, from probably scrambling over everyone else in the room to get out the door first, what exactly would you do?

Would you react violently towards that Celestial Being? Would you admonish that Ethereal Spirit? Would you criticise this Heavenly Entity? I don't think so!

So how would you react? I'll tell you how you would react. You would be in absolute and total awe and wonder! You would be speechless in your amazement! You would feel humbled and honoured that this magnificent Ethereal Being has manifested in front of you! How awesome! What a privilege! And you would kneel in veneration and respect.

Yet! And here is the point we must all take in, each and every one of us! Each and every one of us, without exception, here on this earth, as elsewhere, is a spark of that exact same Divine Essence. And look how we treat each other! We criticise; we judge; we manipulate; we kill; we torture; we maim; we imprison; we condemn; we insult; - the list goes on!

Why do we treat our fellow humans so abominally? Why do we constantly fail to show respect for one another? And the answer? The answer lies in the way in which we perceive ourselves and all those other human beings; in our very limited perception of them as just a physical body; we constantly fail to recognise the spiritual Divine Essence that is inherent in every living thing.

Seeing and treating ourselves and everyone else as pure Spiritual Light is the key to bringing peace, joy and happiness to Planet Earth. And not only that! It is the key also to our own Spiritual Ascension. Seeing and treating ourselves and everyone else as pure Spiritual Light, God Essence, would mean we would not criticise, we would not judge, we would not find fault; we would send out only pure thoughts of unconditional love. And unconditional love is what love is all about. There can be no other kind of love. Conditional love is not love; it is manipulation. To say to someone that you will love them if they do this, that, or whatever; attaching any kind of conditions to loving someone, is not love. Accepting them as they are, and seeing only the good in them,- that's love; that's unconditional love. And that is the only kind of love there can ever be. That is the kind of love your pet has for you. Your pet does not criticise or judge how you look on the morning after the night before. No matter how unkempt you appear in your hung-over state, no matter how grumpy or unwashed you are, your pet does not even notice! He still curls up beside your unwashed body; he still licks your unwashed feet; he still continues to see you as the perfect being, which of course, you are. That's pure, unconditional love. Your pet is pure Spiritual Light, uncontaminated by the lower human ego-based attributes. And in you, he sees only that same pure, Spiritual Light. Nothing else! Get the message?

We have all come to Planet Earth to serve; to spread love, unconditional love. This is wired and programmed into our spiritual and physical nature. This is how we raise our own spiritual vibration and the collective spiritual consciousness of all humanity. The more an unconditionally loving vibration goes out from each one of us, the more harmonious the universe is.

Service to others is not an option; it is a spiritual and a biological necessity. And why? Because it is in caring for, and showing unconditional love to other people that we feed our Soul, that we serve the Divine. Remember what Christ said? – *"That which you do to the least of these my brethren, you do unto me"*. It cannot be more clear. We are all of the Christ Essence, and we need to start treating each other as such.

We all need each other. We all need each other as we climb the ladder of Ascension. Helping others promotes our own wellness, physical and spiritual. In order to address and heal our own issues, we first need to address and heal others. And why? Because in helping others, we help ourselves. Remember! We are all one. Our own issues and problems are forgotten about as we help others in their need; our body and spirit thrive and flourish when we reach out with caring, compassion and empathy, towards another person. Every single time we reach out to others in their need, we set in motion the inevitable forces in Universal Energy which reverberate back to us in like manner, only multiplied numerous times. What you give out, you receive; - one of the Spiritual Laws of the Universe! And if you send out with unconditional love, with your caring, compassionate actions, it can't get any better! Everyone's a winner!

Mother Teresa wrote:- *"The greatest evil is the lack of love and charity, the terrible indifference towards one's neighbour who lives on the road side, assaulted by exploitation, corruption, poverty and disease"*. We can't all be Mother Teresa, obviously, of course! Otherwise, who would be left for us to be Mother Teresa for? Towards whom could we administer our Mother Teresa brand? Likewise, we can't all go off volunteering for charity work overseas. We would end up all chasing each other round the globe, determined to catch someone we could help. Failed mission, of course, because everyone else would also be on the same search-to-help bid as ourselves! The whole system would fall apart; it just wouldn't work. And you don't need to be the Brains of Britain to work that one out! Mother Teresa was one of those highly evolved souls who answered the call to spread unconditional love to those in dire need, with no strings attached; with no discrepancies or discriminations. That was Mother Teresa's soul type. But we don't all have a similar soul type to Mother Teresa.

Remember, too, we are not in any position to judge the actions of anyone else. Our limited earthly vision does not allow us to see what any other person's blue-print or life plan is. We can't even see our own, never mind anyone else's! That other person's life plan may well be to afford all those around them the opportunity to show love, compassion and kindness, and in doing so, help raise their spiritual vibration.

That homeless man on the street, that drug addict, that alcoholic,- they are all brave generous souls, full of unconditional love for humanity, sacrificing their own comfort in order to afford us the opportunity to learn compassion, tolerance, kindness, forgiveness,- all attributes leading us towards Ascension. We cannot see the whole picture, and so we cannot judge. Our limited human vision does not permit us to see that far; but when we pass back to Spirit, then we will see the whole picture; then we will see the whole canvas, the whole tapestry of life and then we will see the threads that we ourselves have woven into that tapestry; the joy we have spread; the pain we have inflicted.

So do not ignore that homeless person,- he is offering you a beautiful, wonderful gift; the priceless gift of learning unconditional love and compassion, which, after all, we have come here to learn. And spreading love,- that is the part we all, each and every one of us plays in the Divine Plan on Earth. If our job in life is cleaning public toilets, sweeping the streets, clearing rubbish, whatever, - we are here to serve humanity, and to serve with love, in some way or other, and if we fulfil that work, no matter how menial it may be, with love and kindness, then we are playing our part, we are honouring our life blue-print, which we ourselves created before we entered this incarnation. We are cleaning those public toilets for other people; we are collecting that rubbish for other people; making life easier and more pleasant for all. Each and every one of us has the power, the power to change lives through actions of kindness, compassion, non-judgement. We all have a duty, a responsibility, a commitment, to use that power in service to others and to the Divine.

Showing unconditional love means giving that homeless man, regardless of why or for what reason he is homeless, that drug addict, that alcoholic, help in some form or other, and not allowing ourselves to hold back because we might consider them as lazy drop-outs, wasters, sponging off society, or whatever. Remember! Everyone we meet has a message for us, a lesson for us to learn. What that homeless man on the street is saying to you is:

*"Hey, man! Don't you recognise me? Can't you see who I really am? Not this physical body, but my bright spiritual Essence? Have you forgotten the agreement we both made before we came here? Remember that lesson you decided you wanted to learn? The reason I am here, like this? How much longer are you going to keep me in this state? How many more times are you going to walk past me before you learn that lesson? Hey, man! Don't just look the other way again! Don't walk on by! You know me! You know who I am! Why can't you recognise me?"*

How much clearer can it all be? What a great pity, what a lost opportunity, if we fail to recognise the hand stretched out to us, if we fail to respond!

And pre-life Soul contracts are made not only between humans, but also between animals and humans. The recent killing of Cecil the lion was not just a random act of wanton violence or lust for blood. Nothing is ever random. A pre-life contract had been made long ago, already put in place, between the soul energy of Cecil and the soul energy of the Mr. Palmer who shot him, to help end the cruel treatment and killing of big game in Zimbabwe game parks. That killing was just the fulfilling, the carrying out, the enactment of that pre-life agreement. And the result? It brought to world attention, more so than ever before, the cruel, unnecessary killings of big game.

Over a million people signed the petition for Zimbabwe to ban such exploits, and that is exactly what happened. Two days after Cecil's passing, big game hunting was banned in Zimbabwe. And not only that! Most major airlines have refused to transport any more so-called "trophies"; and many gun-holders in America and throughout the entire world have handed in their guns, now realising the cruel depravity of their deeds. The love and light that was beamed across the world to Zimbabwe has resulted in achieving what many people have been striving for years to accomplish. It needed a famous, well-known lion like Cecil and an American to bring that about. See the life-plan of both participants here unfolding? It may well be that Mr. Palmer might now become one of the world's foremost campaigners for protection of big game and the end to their unnecessary killing. Who knows? That is why we cannot judge anyone, because we do not know the whole story; and we should be very careful how we react to it! If we react with condemnation and violence, we are not learning the lessons, and we are achieving nothing.

It is the same with all your pets. You and they have made a pre-life agreement to help each other along the path towards Soul Awareness. Your pets are here to help you through troubled times in your life, and when they have seen you through, then it is their time to exit. Your energies will merge again in a joyful re-union, when you yourself pass back to Spirit, where they will be waiting for you, to welcome you home. Is that not beautiful and so spiritually up-lifting?

Giving food, clothes, whatever, to those in their need is one way of helping. This way is helping them through impersonal involvement,- leaving a sandwich or cup of soup beside a homeless person, for example. There is another way, however, to show love and caring. How? By personal involvement. Personal involvement means empowering others, encouraging them, praising them, building up their self-confidence, their esteem,  respecting and listening to their opinions, acknowledging their talents, their abilities, showing belief in them when they have lost all belief in themselves. What strong, empowering acts of service we can all do! And it costs us nothing!

We all play many parts in our life-time, as we learn from the melancholy Jaques, in Shakespeare's "As You Like It":

*"All the world's a stage, / And all the men and women in it merely players;/ They have their exits and their entrances,/ And one man in his time plays many parts".*

That woman sitting beside you on the bus is a daughter, a sister, a mother, a wife, a grand-mother, a nurse, a teacher, a friend, whatever. Likewise, that man sitting on your other side is a son, a father, a grand-father, a soldier, a doctor, a friend, whatever. So you see, in all the inter-related roles we play in our life-time, we are afforded endless opportunities to grow, through showing kindness, compassion, non-judgement, and giving unconditional love, in both our personal and impersonal involvement with all those around us.

Remember, it is not the job or work that we do that is so important; it's how we do it. Doing our work with unconditional love, interspersed with random acts of kindness, negates all the lower based attributes, raises our vibration and brings spiritual growth for us all, for our Planet, and for the entire Universe.

And unconditional love is inextricably bound up with forgiveness and non-judgement; forgiveness and non-judgement are inherent in unconditional love. Loving one another means total forgiveness; loving one another means holding no resentment; and forgiveness and holding no resentment are vital ingredients for strong healthy earthly relationships, and ultimately a peaceful transition back to Spirit. We are all unified from the same Divine Wholeness, the same Divine Oneness, that will, in due time, create universal and eternal peace and love.

Likewise, we need to forgive ourselves. When we forgive ourselves, we free ourselves from that emotion; we release the burden of carrying around with us that resentment, that anger, that hatred, those negative, crippling emotions, which, if not released, will impede our evolutionary process.

When you do extend the hand of forgiveness, unconditional love and caring, either in impersonal or personal involvement forms, do not publicise it, or boast or brag about it, looking for acclaim. That gets you only short-lived rewards in this life-time, so no spiritual brownie points for that one, I'm afraid! Constantly we hear of famous people donating to charities, or setting up sponsorships. Mostly publicity stunts, unfortunately! Genuine, heartfelt unconditional love asks for no return, no acknowledgement, no accolades, no thanks, no publicity, not even a receipt. And that is why we never hear about the vast majority of highly evolved souls on Planet Earth who are working quietly, anonymously and tirelessly, in their own daily work, for the betterment of all humanity, in all parts of the earth. These are the ones who fully understand the meaning of unconditional love, the meaning of Christ's commandment to us; "Love one another!"

# Chapter 12

# Man cannot live on bread alone

I invite you to begin reading this chapter by, again, focusing on the same basic principle, the same basic premise, the same basic foundation stone for all our thoughts and actions. And what, once again, is that basic principle? Once again, that same basic principle that underpins everything we are, everything we do and everything we think, is that we are not just a physical body, but a spiritual body, part of Divine Essence, wrapped in a physical body for the duration of this lifetime only. Each and every one of us is a spirit, encased in a physical body. When we exit this incarnation, our body decomposes and decays, but our Spirit, that Divine part of us, that eternal Soul, moves on to a different level of conscious awareness.

We are all, obviously, very aware of our physical body. But we also have an emotional, a mental, and a spiritual body, not just so obvious to our limited human perception, and therefore, all the more inclined to be ignored more so than our physical body. The many of us who are dedicated to nourishing, maintaining and nurturing our physical body, pampering, decorating, painting, cutting, nicking, tucking! Yet that is the part of us that is going to decay! Our spiritual body is for ever, yet we mostly ignore it, depriving it of nourishment and nurturing, even denying its very existence! How short-sighted is that? Blind, totally!

We need food; of course we do! Food to nourish and maintain our physical body; and food is one of the pleasures of life, to be enjoyed. That's the explanation of the "bread" part. Our body is, after all, the temporary vehicle, the "temple", to transport our immortal Soul through this lifetime. But we also need to nourish and nurture our spiritual body, that part of us that is indissoluble, eternal, everlasting.

And just how do we do that? Where do we find the metaphorical "bread" for that? How do we nurture and sustain that part of us?

We nurture and sustain our Divine Spiritual Essence, first of all, through showing unconditional love, through acts of kindness, caring, compassion, serving humanity with joy and happiness.

But that is not all!

We nourish, nurture and feed our Divine Spiritual Essence through enjoying life, through doing what we love doing, what we are passionate about, and loving what we do. It really is that simple! There is nothing difficult or complicated about it. We have not been asked to trudge our way through life, suffering untold misery after misery, day after day. Doing what we love doing, doing what we are passionate about, - that is how we connect to Spirit, to the Universal Energy, to All That Is. And when we are connected to Spirit, our Soul is thriving.

We all make that connection to Spirit in a different way. A musician connects through his or her music; a painter through paintings; a dancer through dancing. All of these connect in a different way, but they all have one thing in common, – their love of what they do and the joy they get from doing it. It is that love that makes their Soul fly freely; it is that love that creates the feeling of elation. And when your Soul is singing and flying freely, you are connected to Divine Spirit; and when you are connected to Divine Spirit, you are nourishing and feeding your Soul.

All forms of creativity,- visual, performing, or literary,- go hand in hand with Spirituality. Remember how I explained Spirituality?

Spirituality is an awareness that there is something far greater than we are, something that created the Universe, created life, and that we are an authentic, important, significant part of it, and can contribute to its evolution. All of us, when we were born from Source, from God, were endowed with a facet of Divinity. That means, in a very literal sense, that we have a part of that Source within us. That is what gives us the knowledge of our immortality. And that is what connects us to Universal Intelligence. All artists, in whatever field, and the Universal Creative Intelligence, are one. All creativity, no matter what, awakens the consciousness of the Creator within us. All forms of creativity explore and see the world and all creation in new, fresh, or unprecedented ways, and when we see the world and all creation in new, fresh, or unprecedented ways, a moment of Awakening of Consciousness occurs. All the great artists, musicians, writers, performers, have opened our eyes to the beauty of the world. All of these recognise that the same Force that creates the flowers, trees, galaxies, also creates art form through the creative artist. Divine Intelligence connects with us and talks to us through art, music and all forms of creativity. And not only do all of these express the beauty of the world; they also express the darker side of humanity, evoking our compassion and caring. For example, a monument to the victims of some particular disaster, or a piece of literature exploring some human situation, feelings or emotions. Graffitti or other forms of art designed to stir up hatred or revenge, however, do not inspire, only incite, and that is not connection to Source or spirituality.

Feeding your Soul is not an option; your Soul cries out for nourishment; and you have a duty to feed it, by doing what resonates with your inner spiritual being. We have all, at some time or another, experienced that high, that exhilaration, that comes with doing something we love doing. That is you feeding and nourishing your Soul. So just keep on doing it, whatever it may be. Just as long, of course, as it causes no pain to yourself, to any other human being, or to any other form of life. You do not need the artificial stimulants of drugs or alcohol to experience that elation. They only feed your immediate physical desires; they do not nourish your Soul. Neither are there sufficient words to describe that feeling you experience; it is a spiritual feeling, not a physical feeling. Your Soul cries out for sustenance, and in having fun, enjoying life, being happy, you are nourishing your Soul. Again, it's something so simple, that it's often overlooked or misunderstood. We are meant to be happy; it is our natural birth-right, and in being happy, having fun, we are feeding our soul. Man cannot live on bread alone, simply because there is a lot more to him than just his physical body, and bread feeds only that physical body, not his immortal spiritual body. That spiritual body also needs feeding, nurturing and sustenance. And how easy that becomes, when you know how!

# Chapter 13

# There Are Many Mansions in My Father's House

What exactly do these words mean?

"There are many Mansions in my Father's House" is a direct reference to the Higher Vibrations of pure Light and Energy that we call Heaven, the Celestial Kingdoms, Utopia, Elysium, the Spirit World, Happy Hunting Grounds, whatever.

The word "Mansions" simply means levels. Levels of what? Levels of spiritual awareness; levels of soul consciousness; levels of raised vibration. Each mansion represents a higher level of consciousness of our Divine nature and our indissoluble connection with Spirit. In the process of a soul's awakening, that soul progresses through many mansions, each containing many rooms, some for specific purposes, others for general purposes; but all with a particular theme for learning in each soul's eternal process of evolution and expansion, from soul immaturity to higher understanding. Each soul progresses through these various levels, as each soul, together with all of humanity, and the greater Universe, all seek elevation, Ascension and spiritual advancement.

There are not just two levels of existence, "this" side and the "other" side. Far from it! As above, so below; as below, so above. We all have different levels of perception on "this" side, where we can all experience the same event, but we may have very different reactions, depending on our interpretation, understanding and impact, because of our different levels of perception. How often have you asked someone "What planet are you on?" or "What wave-length are you on?" indicating that someone is not seeing from your own particular perspective? These varying levels of consciousness exist in the Spirit World as well. Even Angels and Spirit Guides vibrate at different spiritual levels, different spiritual frequencies, based on their own levels of spiritual attainment, as they too are evolving, their attainment levels based on how well they do their job with us. Our Spirit Guides and Angels need us as much as we need them, because at any particular point in time, their reason for their very existence is to help and guide us. They are no better or greater than us in the whole Divine equation, the whole Divine network, the whole Divine Plan; they have just progressed further along their own spiritual path, and we are all on that same spiritual road back to Source. We are all simply energy, vibrating at different frequencies. In fact, the Angels look on us with the same amazement and awe as we do them!

Like Shakespeare's Hamlet, we have all questioned the existence of an after-life and wondered what it is:

*"To be or not to be..........that is the question. / To die, to sleep; / To sleep, perchance to dream: ay, there's the rub; / For in that sleep of death what dreams may come , / When we have shuffled off this mortal coil, / Must give us pause."*

Hamlet is questioning, as we have all done, if dying is the end or is it akin to going to sleep?

To answer this, we must, first of all, understand that eternity is not something that begins after death and goes on from there for ever and ever. We do not have to die to experience the afterlife and eternity. We are already in eternity, here and now! This is the Eternal Now! And that's all there can ever be! And this life-time is just one of the numerous phases of our long walk-about across eternity, as our soul continues to learn and expand, always in need of gaining further awareness. Passing back to Spirit as we exit this incarnation is simply the door to our next phase of our soul's profound climb to higher wisdom and knowledge, in just the same way as being born into this earthly existence is also just a door into another stage of this continuous quest and striving for soul advancement. So you see, we are in eternity now, in this, just one of the numerous phases of our existence as some form of energy, and energy is all there is; everything is energy, vibrating at different levels, soul energy being a light frequency compared to our much more dense physical bodily energy.

When we exit this incarnation, our soul gravitates towards a particular level or plane. As your soul leaves your physical body, the silver cord connecting your soul to your body breaks, and as you pass through the White Light, you automatically switch on to auto-pilot. Your soul knows instinctively where to go, what to do. After all, you have come from here many times before, and you have experienced this return journey, this returning home, many, many times before! Everything is familiar, now that you have passed through the veil of amnesia, once again. That memory has been locked into your subconscious, but now, once again, becomes available to you at your time of crossing, removing all fear, the bright energy giving you a cleansing feeling, as it adjusts to your own particular spiritual vibration, to be compatible with whatever spiritual level you have attained. It is a very smooth transition in all cases, because it is guided solely by what each mind is ready for. There is no dense physical accompanying body to interfere with the transmission of energy, as you merge with the other pure energy senses around you, gravitating automatically to your own spiritual level of attainment and level of consciousness, all souls gravitating into homogeneous groups according to the rate of each soul's vibration. There is no discomfort or shock associated with crossing over, as each soul is asked to handle only that which it is capable of handling, according to its own spiritual development.

The various after-life realms are like different frequencies in the light spectrum, invisible to the naked human eye. They are not a "place" as we know a place to be here on earth, but vibrations: vibrations of light; vibrations of colour; vibrations of energy. Neither are these levels suspended in mid-air. Far from it! They are supported by an energy field that we cannot possibly perceive with our human, limited earthly vision; that we cannot possibly see from our own present level of energy. Earth gravity does not apply. All those who have had a Near Death Experience report a change in vibrational frequency, allowing them to experience a sense of space, liberation, infinity, and an all-knowingness. There is no containment or limitation whatsoever, no walls, no barriers, no dense objects of any kind, no sense of time or linear progression; only a sense of peaceful floating in a timeless, unrestricted zone.

Soul energy is a light frequency, perceived as colour. The after-life is a multi-dimensional reality, full of exploding colours and light frequencies, much like the Aurora Borealis, only magnified millions of times. All the different colours indicate how developed and how spiritually aware each soul is at this particular stage in their spiritual progression. The highest plane of all is where you reach total Enlightenment, Nirvana, exemplified in the figurine of the Reclining Buddha.

And what determines which level each of us gravitates towards, which level each of us will find ourselves on, when we pass over back to Spirit?

The particular level at which each of us arrives is determined by the kind of life we lived while here on the earth plane, this time around, and how successful we have been in fulfilling our life's plan; how well we have learned and incorporated the lessons we came here to learn.

We take with us from this life-time, or from any other previous life-time, no earthly possessions, no material goods, no earthly accolades. As the poet Francis Beaumont wrote in "On the Tombs in Westminster Abbey":

*"Though Gods they were, as men they died."*

So also the poet James Shirley, writing at the time of the English Civil War in the mid seventeenth century, explained:

*"The glories of our blood and state / Are shadows, not substantial things"* and *"Only the actions of the just / Smell sweet and blossom in the dust".*

Nevertheless, we do not go completely empty-handed. We do need the metaphorical passport; and in that passport we have got all the brownie points, all the tokens, all the vouchers that we have managed to collect whilst we were here on earth.

If we are going on holiday, or on any journey, we usually make some preparations; get a map, learn something about the place, check the weather, decide what we need. We draw up a plan of action. So it is when we cross over, back to Spirit. We are going to Spirit, so we need spiritual things. We need to be prepared! We need our spiritual vouchers, we need all the brownie points we can get, we need those spiritual tokens. And we have to earn them before we go!

So where do we get these vital vouchers? How do we collect these obligatory tokens? How can we earn those necessary brownie points?

All of us here on Planet Earth have willingly undertaken to be here at this point in time, to help in raising the consciousness of all humanity, bringing Planet Earth into a new, higher vibration. Each of us has undertaken a unique role to play in fulfilling our life-time mission this time around. When our earthly existence comes to an end and we cross back to Spirit, there is no judgement, no condemnation, no recriminations. There are no scales, weighing up our good deeds and our not-so-good deeds, and then some Deity on High pointing us in a particular direction, to eternal punishment or to eternal reward. No! Rather, we face our own life review; we ourselves decide how well or how ineffectively we learned the lessons we came here to learn. And it is in the process of learning these lessons that we ourselves have chosen to learn, that we collect our tokens, vouchers and brownie points,- our passport to our own particular level in the next phase of our eternal existence.

The well-known English contemporary poet, actor and dramatist Heathcote Williams, one of today's strongest voices against planetary destruction and social injustice, has explained how *"death develops life's photographs."* Death holds up to us a mirror that shows us everything from our lives, *"the mirror of past actions",* and as we once again witness all of this, in our own life review, we see the consequences of all our positive actions, and the consequences of all our less-than-positive actions. All of these actions, good and bad, are now seen by us clearly in the light of their consequences, and how they affected other people. If we hurt or offended any other form of life, we will now experience that same feeling that we perpetrated on them, and, likewise, when we brought joy or happiness to any other person, through positive, loving actions, we will now feel how we made them feel. So death, as we see it, is like a photographic processing of our entire life, where we re-experience all of our own actions, in multi-dimensional form.

In this post-mortem state, as we review our life's actions and, more importantly, the consequences of all our life's actions, our soul automatically gravitates towards the level of transference of consciousness for which we ourselves have prepared while we were here in this life-time. And it is here, in this life-time, that we collect our credits, balance our spiritual accounts, and earn our level in the

Spirit World. So it is absolutely imperative that we take responsibility for our own actions, and that we understand the consequences of all our actions. And why? Because it is on that understanding that our level of attainment when we cross over, depends. It is too late then to try to make amends or wish we had done things differently. But remember! There is no such thing as failure! All is not lost; all is never lost in Spirit. We will be given chance after chance, again and again, to improve our performance, to come round again and again, if we so wish, to learn those lessons properly. What lessons? Those lessons we ourselves freely chose to learn while in this life-time; the experiences we chose to undergo to learn those lessons, the lessons of serving humanity and spreading unconditional love and happiness, raising our own vibration, and the collective spiritual consciousness of all humanity.

So, what do we actually do when we cross over? How do we spend our "time"? What is it like on the "other" side of the veil of amnesia? What is it like in these "Mansions"? What goes on there?

When we pass back to Spirit, we are not just sitting around all day and night on a fluffy cloud, playing the harp or singing hymns. Hardly! First of all, there is no day or night; there is no time as we know it to be here on earth. It is the rotation of the earth on its tilted axis that creates day and night for us here. But when in Spirit, we are not on any planet. We are in a dimension, a frequency, an energy vibration much lighter and higher than when we were here on earth, a new consciousness awareness. We are always evolving as spiritual beings, and we continue our evolutionary process in this new consciousness awareness, back with Spirit, from the vantage point of having discarded our earthly, human limitations. We are now solely involved and occupied with feeding and nourishing our soul. We no longer need to feed and nourish our physical body. And why not? Simply because we no longer have one! It was always only temporary.

This is now solely soul-replenishing time, solely soul re-energising time, solely soul re-charging time. Our soul constantly thirsts, hungers and yearns for growth and knowledge, and this is now soul's time to satisfy all that thirst, all that hunger, all that yearning.

The After-life is filled with love and joy far beyond anything we can comprehend on this earthly plane. And as we ascend up through the spiritual levels, learning the lessons and gaining knowledge, our soul rejoices, basks and luxuriates in growth and healing. Yes! Our learning to love and grow continues in the Spiritual Realms.

As above, so below. When we cross over back to Spirit, we do not suddenly undergo a complete personality transformation; nor do we suddenly become a truly enlightened being, or an Angel or a Saint, carrying a huge big halo on the top of our head! Rather, we retain our individual traits and eccentricities, as we continue to evolve, as totally spiritual beings now, no longer also physical beings, strengthening our connection to Spirit through continuing to enjoy what we enjoyed doing while on the earth plane. If music, for example, was our love here on earth, then we continue to enjoy that, but now perhaps inspiring others on earth to develop their interest or skills in music, or perhaps helping someone compose some beautiful melody or some particular piece of music that we didn't manage to do while we were here. All the great works of art, all the great symphonies, - they all originated in Spirit. All the great inventions, likewise, were all instilled and inspired into the minds of people on earth by those already in the After-life. So, from your vantage point in Spirit, you are still helping humanity to evolve and increase soul awareness, because remember, all forms of creativity and spirituality go together, hand in hand. What you are doing is awakening the Universal Creative Intelligence in people on earth, awakening people's awareness of beauty in the world, and awakening their connection to their Divine Essence. A lot more productive than sitting around on a fluffy cloud all day playing a harp or singing hymns!

Just as there are many grade levels of learning and achievement in schools here on earth, so too in the Afterlife. When we arrive at our attained level of soul awareness, we continue to learn and grow in the various healing rooms, and all the diverse types of learning places. This life-time on earth is just one grade of the whole process, and just as we progress on earth through learning, so too, we progress up through all the levels in the Spirit World, according to our accomplishments. And just as we have people here on earth who are accomplished in their own particular field, in the material world, so also in the Spirit World. However, the fact that some have progressed further than others on their spiritual awareness path, does not make any of these superior or greater than any other. We are all, as souls, in charge of our own destiny. I might not regard myself as having your wisdom, your mental capacity, or whatever. But I'm your equal in Spirit! There are no superior beings. And why not? Simply because we are all one! There is no separation! I am you and you are me. So how can there be levels of superiority or inferiority in that? There can't!

The spiritual realms are highly structured and ordered, with the constant onward movement of souls towards Ascension; the schools of learning; the healing rooms; even the nurseries, where souls are prepared for re-entry into this earthly dimension. And there is no incarnate evil! Despite what we have been led to believe, every soul entering this incarnation is born as pure Divine Light, uncontaminated, unsullied, untarnished. And again, contrary to what we have been led to believe, there is no place of punishment called Hell. Each and every soul will, ultimately, arrive back at Source. Of course, there are darker energies, at a very low stage of their soul evolution, but even they, too, are on the upward moving Cosmic Escalator.

When we arrive at our own particular level in the Spirit World, what happens if our loved ones are on a different level, a higher or a lower level than us, as may well be the case? Do we get to see them? How do we meet up with them?

In answer to this, - remember, they are not in any other place. They are all, like us, energy; energy vibrating at different frequencies. We don't get to hug them, as such, because we have no physical body with which to hug them. But! We do get to merge our energy with theirs, in a glorious, happy re-union, any time we want. There is no language barrier in the Spirit World; everything and every thought is instantly manifested through telepathy and mind and thought consciousness processing. If we are on the lower level of vibration and our loved ones are on the higher, we cannot access their level. And why not? Because we have not yet earned that level! That's the bad news. And the good news?  Higher level souls can transcend to the lower levels to facilitate a meeting, through instant thought processing. So yes, our loved ones are always around us and instantly available to us in the Spirit World.

And not just in the Spirit World! Those of our loved ones who have already passed over to Spirit are not in another place; just in a different energy frequency, and available to us at all times, literally only a thought away. To manifest in front of us, though, takes a lot of energy on their part, because earth energy is so dense, and often it can only happen if another soul joins energy with the soul wishing to manifest for a loved one still here on the earth plane. When my own mother first came to me, she was joined by her mother and a cousin. It is much easier for souls in Spirit to move things about, or to turn off the electricity, for example, to get your attention, just to let you know they are present, as it requires much less energy on their part. When my father passed away, over forty years ago now, I remember my mother and I were sitting at the fireside one afternoon, just a few weeks after his passing. There were china cups and saucers sitting on the table behind us. The sound of a spoon being set down on a china saucer is a very clear, distinct, unmistakable sound. And it was that clear, distinct, unmistakable sound that my mother and I both heard on that occasion. Just my father telling us, "I'm fine! I'm still with you! I haven't gone anywhere!"

Likewise, when my mother passed back to Spirit a few years ago, I got very strong, clear signs from her immediately after her passing. As we were all gathered around her hospital bedside, just before the end, I asked the Angels to get me just a few minutes with her on my own. Almost immediately, nurses came in and asked us to leave for a short time to enable them to make my mother more comfortable. I hung around outside the door, and as soon as they came out, I darted in. I bent down over her head and whispered in her ear that it was time for her to go, her family in Spirit were gathered, waiting to greet her on the other side. I thanked her for being my mum, and asked her to give me a ring when she was safely over. I told her to keep going toward the Light and to not look back, everything was as it should be. Her head inclined ever so slightly towards my forehead, and I knew she had heard me. She left this incarnation less than an hour afterwards, with a final deep, peaceful sigh, as her soul exited to its next stage of evolution. When I returned home that evening, the knob on the top of my bed post was missing, and despite searching high and low, I failed to locate it. Next day, when her coffin was being taken out from the Undertaker's, the sky was blue, and suddenly, down in front of her coffin fluttered three little white feathers. My first sign! After the funeral, when I returned home again, the scent of white lilies flooded my sitting room. We had placed only white lilies on her coffin. My second sign! Next morning, a huge butterfly scraped its way down my conservatory window several times, and even though the windows were all open, it did not come in. It fluttered about for a considerable time and then flew off. My third sign! And my fourth sign? When I went upstairs, there, lying on the ground, between the bed and the door, where I could not possibly have failed to see it, was the missing knob! Even if I had been totally blind, I would have stepped on it!

I have had several more signs from my mother since her passing. In fact, she continues to let me know she is still around, looking after us all from her vantage point in Spirit, seeing the whole picture, which we cannot see. The first New Year's Eve after her passing, the solar lights in my garden lit up at exactly midnight, for just a few minutes. Solar lights lighting up at midnight at the darkest time of the year! How did that happen?  Next morning, I rang my friend, Spiritual Medium Margaret Hurdman, who immediately said it was my mother. I asked for some sort of proof. Margaret's answer? "Why is your mother telling me the lights in your garden are blue and white?" Yes! That was true! But I needed more. The next response? "Who had the sick stomach yesterday?" Yes, I had! That was the reason I was house- bound on New Year's Eve! Still not convinced, I tried again. And Margaret's response this time? "No more tears, Eileen!" Yes! I had shed a lot of tears for my mother the previous day! So how can I possibly doubt that my mother was making contact with me on that occasion? Margaret could not possibly have known any of those things!

Just recently, the numbers 77 have been popping up in front of me. My father passed in '77 and my mother on the 7th day of the 7th month. It seems more than just what many would call coincidence, that nearly every car number plate to which my eyes are drawn contains the numbers 77!  I leave you to decide for yourself!

And it is not just our own departed loved ones who are around us. Other spirits who want to get messages through to their loved ones are always waiting for their chance, indeed even steering us in a certain direction to deliver their message for them. When I was recording my first cd, "Celestial Healing", we were interrupted about ten minutes into the recording by a mobile phone ringing. I did not have my phone with me, so it definitely was not mine! The other mobile in the studio was on silent, but it managed to ring. We started again, and at exactly the same place, the same phone rang again. A slight suspicion crossed my mind that someone was trying to tell someone something; but we finished the recording without further incident. Next morning, I was due to return to record my second cd, "Celestial Presence". I had used the Tibetan bowls in the first cd and I asked for some sort of sign as to whether I should use my chimes for the second one. No sign came. When I returned to the recording studio next morning, I was informed that my chimes had been playing through the house for a while during the night, and the television and lights in the sitting room had turned themselves on! There was my sign! Decision made! Chimes to be included in cd! But that's not where this story ends! Far from it! The following Saturday I was due in Dreamcatchers Holistic Center, Mairead Murray's beautiful Angel shop in Cavan, for the launching of my book and cds. Mairead's sister, Patricia Kierans, had passed to Spirit just two years previously in violent circumstances. As the cd was playing, and the chimes pealed out, Mairead informed me that after her sister had passed, she had gone to a spiritual medium to connect with her. And the message she got from her sister? "Listen for the chimes!" It was a very emotional moment, but very beautiful. This all just goes to show how those in Spirit can see everything from their vantage point, and can pick their moment to make themselves known to us in order to get their message to their loved ones! I now know whose energy turned that phone on, turned the television and lights on, and turned the chimes on! Again, I leave you to make your own mind up on that one! It's like a game of chess! And we are the pawns! We are being moved about! But! It's all good!

Yes! Our departed loved ones and all others in Spirit are always around us, continuing to watch over us from their vantage point in Spirit. And yes! They do try to connect with us from time to time. We just need to watch for the signs: white feathers; robins or any other birds; butterflies; a particular familiar piece of music suddenly catching your attention; a particular scent; something being said or talked about when you turn on your television or radio; the words of a song; a message on a billboard; something someone says to you; objects being moved; lights flickering; electricity being turned off; a recurring piece of music, - these are all possible signs from your loved ones in the After-life. But remember, they also have their own "lives" to be getting on with; they are busy doing other things, so we should respect that and let them get on with it and not be bothering them all the time. They are evolving in their own way; maybe acting as guides for others here on earth; helping souls cross over; helping darker energies towards the Light; healing; whatever. And they are also enjoying life! Parties, celebrations, festivities, concerts,- you name it, they have it! Maybe your departed loved one is already back in another incarnation here on Planet Earth. The list of possibilities as to what they could be doing is endless! And their main message to all of us always is to get on with our lives, to be happy, do the best we can, and attain the highest level we can for when we, too, arrive back in the Spirit World, where they will be waiting for us, waiting to welcome us home, and there will be a glorious re-uniting in the merging of our energies; a great big spiritual hug! And maybe a white fluffy cloud to float about on!

Yes! The physical and spiritual realms are all one! There is no separation! As above, so below; as below, so above.

# Chapter 14

# Do Not Be Afraid!

Everything, absolutely everything in our lives comes to us at the right time. Indisputable! One of the Spiritual Laws of the Universe!

The Universe knows all our needs and caters for them. Indisputable! Another of the Spiritual Laws of the Universe!

And there is nothing, absolutely nothing to fear. Everything is Divinely time-coded and Divinely arranged. And we must accept that, if we are to live happily, free from worry and fear. The Cosmos is completely self-correcting, adjusting to and manifesting our every need; and so are we. All we have to do is surrender our individual will to Divine Will.

Love! The regulatory energy of the entire Universe! The strongest, most positive of all forces! And the most destructive force? Hatred, which we would call the direct opposite of love? Actually, no! It is fear that is the most destructive, negative force. And why? Because all negative forces and emotions, including hatred itself, stem from fear. If we could rid the world of just one thing, then let that one thing be fear, and we would have Heaven on Earth! And it is through fear that the mass of humanity is, and always has been, controlled and manipulated. All the conditioning, all the beliefs which have fenced mankind in have created fear for century after century.

Fear causes wars, aggression, greed, arrogance, envy, jealousy,- all the lower based attributes that keep so many people stuck in the lower vibrational levels.

And why is fear so poisonous? Because it paralyses us, it diminishes us, it sabotages who we are. It inhibits our souls from singing and flying freely; it prevents us from reaching our full potential. And we all feel it at some time or another. Even the most evil amongst us! Shakespeare's Macbeth, for all his bravado, all his terrorising, all his murdering, experienced fear:

*"But now I am cabined, cribbed, confined, bound in / To saucy doubts and fears."*

James Joyce, in his collection of short stories, "Dubliners", has very effectively portrayed the negativity incumbent in fear, in all its aspects. Joyce's central concern in "Dubliners" was the paralysis that he saw limiting and frustrating the lives of the people of Dublin. He himself wrote: *"My intention was to write a chapter of the moral history of my country, and I chose Dublin for the scene because that city seemed to me to be the centre of paralysis. I have tried to present.........four of its aspects: childhood, adolescence, maturity, and public life."*

Joyce himself admitted that the picture of the Irish people he has drawn is not a flattering one: *"It is not my fault that the odour of ashpits and old weeds and offal hangs around my stories."* He presents a series of studies of the effects of paralysis through fear on the lives of individual Dubliners, tracing the effects through childhood, adolescence, and into maturity and old age.

"The Sisters" is one of these short stories from Joyce's "Dubliners". Here, Father Flynn was paralysis itself, a broken man, broken and paralysed physically, mentally and spiritually, symbolic of the Church with its empty rituals and rigid institutions. The old priest has lost his faith and with it, his priestly role, afraid to look for an escape route. Paralysed through fear!

In another of Joyce's short stories, "Eveline", the main character, Eveline, is nineteen years old. She leads a hard and routine life, with a job she does not enjoy, running the family home since her mother died and looking after her aggressive, alcoholic father. She is offered the chance of escape by Frank, and a new life in a foreign country, but Eveline's fear of the unknown, her inability to break from everything she has ever known, leaves her in a state of fear and total paralysis. Her underlying instinct is to stay and fulfil her duty as a daughter, as society dictates, but her conscious desire is to leave, to start a new life with Frank. The ingredients of her paralysis are a drunken father; poverty; the pervasive influence of religion, and the expectations of society. The influences of her environment are too strong for her to break, and her fear keeps her in her paralysed state of existence. Paralysed through fear!

Yet again, in "A Little Cloud", a third example from "Dubliners", Little Chandler feels himself trapped and his creativity stifled by his own timidity and his circumstances. To Chandler, his old friend, Gallaher, has become a "brilliant figure", casting off his "shabby and necessitous guise", to make his way in London, in a successful career. But Chandler, in his paralysis, is afraid and unable to move outside his own limited mediocrity, a victim of fear and all its paralysing entourage. Paralysed through fear!

We need to break free from fear, from whatever source it is coming. Fear suffocates our soul, it stifles our creativity, it denies us our freedom. People who speak negatively of us, making us feel we are "no good", we are "just a waste of space", we have "nothing to contribute", are operating through the medium of fear in order to project their own feelings on to us, to feed their own deflated ego. What we see and criticise in others is a direct reflection of what we see in ourselves. So their criticisms, their judgements of us say more about them than they do about us. Our outside world is an exact reflection of our inner world. As within, so without.

We all have tremendous power within us, each and every one of us; power to change society; power to over-ride fear; power to bring about good. Fear that we will be mocked, scoffed at, laughed at, scorned, ridiculed; fear that we will not be good enough; fear that we will fail; fear that we are going against the dictates of society, or Church, all keep us in a paralysis of our soul. Failure? Remember! There is no such thing! So how can anyone be afraid of something that never has, and never will, exist?

Fear has been instilled into us from all time, down through every generation. Think of all the evil creeds there have been in the world, and the methods they all used to control nations. Yes! Fear! "Animal Farm", a political satire by George Orwell, on the Communist regime in Russia, fully epitomises the methods such regimes use in order to control. The pigs control all the other animals through fear: instilling fear of the vicious specially-trained dogs; playing on their fear of the return of Jones, to manipulate them to work harder and harder, but all only for the benefit of the pigs themselves, the ruling party. All exploiters are the same. They find a weakness, a fear, and then they gain control through manipulating that fear. It's all around us: in governments; in state institutions; in financial institutions; in church institutions.

Our thoughts create our reality. The thoughts we send out attract similar to us. Fear based emotions create a fear based vibration that only causes even more chaos and confusion in your life and in the world. Every feeling of fear we send out only serves to actually draw that which we fear, to us. Remember, the Universe re-arranges itself to reflect our reality. When we fear for tomorrow, what it will, or will not bring, we are not living as we should be, in total trust that the Universe knows what we need and desire, and will deliver. That is what Christ meant by "Fear not". The birds, the trees, all in Nature do not worry, fear or fret, they "just be", and so should we, knowing that there is a Universal Force, far greater than us, providing all our needs. By being afraid, by worrying or fretting, we are going against the Universal flow, and we are actually hindering or impeding the flow to us of what we desire.

Think about it! When we hear that there is going to be a petrol shortage, or a delivery strike, what do we all do? Rush to the nearest filling station with cans, canisters, buckets, anything we can find, and fill up with petrol. And what happens? The petrol supply runs out! Of course it does! How could it not? If we just went about our ordinary every-day business calmly, just buying as we need, and not starting to panic or fear, there would be enough for everyone. Again, if we get any sort of notion that the banks are going to run out of money, what do we all do? Run to the bank and withdraw all our money. Result? Exactly! The banks run out of money! The same when we hear about a shortage of food. We create that shortage ourselves by stocking up and hoarding far more than is necessary for our immediate needs. What are we like?

Just go with the flow. The flow of what? The flow of Divine Universal Energy! Let it all happen, allow everything to unfold as Divine Energy intends. As John Lennon, in his famous song, wrote:

*"In times of trouble, Mother Mary comes to me, speaking words of wisdom, 'Let it be, let it be'".*

Words of wisdom indeed! If only we would listen! Letting things flow, accepting what happens as always being for our highest good, and is always Divinely guided and monitored, negates all fear on our part, all soul paralysis. We are asked to just trust; trust in Divine Spirit; trust in the omniscient, omnipotent and omnipresent Higher Force that has everything, absolutely everything, under Divine control and in Divine order. Everything, absolutely everything that we need, will come to us, not when we dictate it, force it, or manipulate it, but in Divine timing, in Divine place and in Divine way. It is our own lower based ego, our fear, that tries to make us go it alone, that tries to produce the outcome we want, and not the outcome Spirit has intended for us, all for our own highest good.

Everything happens for a reason and a purpose. If you lose your house through mortgage payment default, or if you are made redundant, or if someone close to you is terminally ill, whatever, these are all happening for a reason. What do you have to do? Think, and look for that reason! As Lewis Carroll wrote: *"Everything has a moral; if only we could find it!"* We are constantly being guided back on to our pre-life blue-print, through the lessons afforded us, and, after all, we ourselves created that! That's what having free will means; the complete freedom to create our own life-plan. And when we are here, we can still exert our free will to step out of that plan at any time, to deviate from the path. In that case, all that happens is that our Spirit Guides and Angels simply keep putting events and people in front of us to direct us back on to that path, the path we ourselves drew up for ourselves, this time around. So remember! Everything that happens to you, you yourself have freely chosen to happen! We have all created our own blue-print, and so we are bound to face it!

Always, always, all is well. We are always in the right place, at the right time. We often hear, when an accident or what we call an "accident" occurs, or some tragedy, how someone was in the wrong place at the wrong time. Such a situation can never be! Everything that happens is meant to happen, it is meant to "be". We cannot make a mistake, simply because there is no such thing as a mistake, ever! All are learning experiences. We cannot get something wrong, simply because there is no such thing as getting something "wrong". And we cannot fail, simply because again, there is no such thing as "failure"; never has been, never will be. Learning that lesson is simply a matter of timing, and we will learn it, no matter how many times it has to keep presenting itself to us in order for us to do so.

So, do not keep beating yourself up or hold on to any feelings of guilt for what you consider to be your "failures". That's just your lower-based ego at work on you again, niggling away at you, gnawing at you, manipulating you. Just tell it buzz off!

Do not be afraid! There is, literally, nothing to fear. Those who criticise or condemn you, for whatever reason, are simply projecting their own fears on to you! They are operating from the lower Third Dimension Vibration. Do not join them down there! They are the ones with the problem, not you! You are just a cog in the wheel, a part of their learning experience. Bless them, send them love, and send them on their way; that is the only way to disarm them. They can only hurt your lower-based pride, and even then, only if you let them; they cannot damage or inflict any hurt or pain on who you really are; - that Spark of the Divine Essence, that immortal part of you that, like the eagle, soars above earthly matters, knowing that all your needs are provided for and will be delivered in Divine timing.

Fear not! There is nothing to fear. You are constantly being looked after and provided for and everything that happens is for your own highest good. Just look for the lesson!

Neither should you fear for your children. Do not fear or worry that they will mess up or get it all wrong. The same rules that apply to you also apply to your offspring. The same laws that apply to you also apply to your offspring. There is no "failure" for them, just as there is no failure for you. There is no getting it wrong for them, just as there is no getting it wrong for you. They have chosen you as their parents this time around in order to learn the lessons they want to learn. This is their life, not yours! You have your own! And that is enough for you to be getting on with! How many more do you want? Leave them to get on with theirs in the way they themselves have decided. You cannot buy their love by promising a reward if they do this, get that, pass their exam, attain that degree, whatever. Of course, encourage and support them, and above all, empower them. But if your son opts out of education and spends years wandering around the globe in order to "find himself" or whatever, then that is his blue-print unfolding, and he has every right to follow that blue-print, which he himself freely created for himself, in just the very same way as you freely created your life blue-print. He has free will, just as you have! And he has lessons to learn, just as you have, but they are different lessons! If the time is not right here and now, for him to pursue further education, when and if he is ever meant to go down that particular path, then it will happen, in Divine timing. Not in your timing but In Divine timing. Not at your command, but In Divine Order.

Likewise, you might well expect your son or daughter to take on your family business, farm, or particular career. Again, it is not your choice! Your free will extends to you yourself only! You cannot have free will for anyone else, or exercise your free will on their behalf! All you are doing is interfering with, impeding their spiritual growth, interfering negatively in this, their pre-life blue-print. You have got to step aside and allow them to find their own path in this, their life, not yours. Manipulating them, coercing them, forcing them, is totally non-productive and non-conducive to their happiness or their spiritual growth.

Nor does your offspring joining your business, just to please and placate you, bring any asset whatsoever to that business. Anything that is undertaken solely as a duty is not spiritually healthy. We are here to raise our own vibration and that of all humanity, by being happy in what we are doing. But if someone goes to work every day, and is not happy about it, then how is that going to raise anyone's vibration? Never mind all of humanity! Only doom and gloom all around! And guess what! That doom and gloom will only attract more doom and gloom! Brilliant!!!

Some people know instinctively what they want to do in life. Others do not. They try this, try that, try everything. But they are not "failing". Failure, again, does not come into the equation, in any way, shape or form. They are having wonderful, amazing, learning experiences, exactly what they came here to find! Perfect! Absolutely perfect! You cannot learn their lessons for them, any more than you would try to learn off a passage of Shakespeare for them. You wouldn't even dream of doing that! Stupid or what? Nor would you ever dream of telling them to study a certain text for an exam, which is not on their syllabus, just because you studied it. Get the message?

Each of your offspring will find his own path in life, and if you show him unconditional love, and leave him to learn his own lessons and find that path, that is exactly what he will do. It is wired and programmed into him. He will learn those lessons, and in doing so, will find happiness in doing what he himself loves doing. That is the real test of you as a parent! Not how many degrees your offspring get, or how many letters they have after their name, or even how much money they make; but in how comfortable, happy and fulfilled they are in their own skin and in their own life.

So be tolerant of what you may see as your "wayward" offspring. "Wayward" by whose standards? Yours? See them as the beautiful, shining, spiritual light they really are, and send them unconditional love. Remember, too, you also have lessons to learn here. Think about it! To be more tolerant? More compassionate? More understanding? To learn to let go? To draw back? To swallow your pride? What was it Lewis Carroll said about everything having a moral? - "You just have to find it!"

Fear dissipates once you accept the part of Spirit in your life, and once you let go of those fears, knowing you are being guided, protected and looked after, synchronicities will flood your existence, as they have done mine. And yes, I said synchronicities, not coincidences. Coincidence? There is no such thing! My own first book, "Living the Magic" is proof of that; evidence of the part played by synchronicity in life! The synchronistic flow of life that comes from releasing your fears and accepting your own Divine connection! Let me explain how my first book materialised!

Every book tells a story and every book has a story, the story of its own conception and birth into the printed word. "Living the Magic" was born out of the most bizarre set of synchronicities; synchronicities so bizarre, that even the strongest sceptic amongst us must pause and ponder, if only for a moment, that perhaps, maybe just perhaps, there might, after all, be a Force greater than us; a Universal Mind; a Power beyond this human dimension; an all-seeing, all-knowing Power, steering us, guiding us, leading us in a direction for our own highest good and the good of all humanity.

At the end of October 2014, I had no idea whatsoever that within the space of just three weeks, I would have a book not only written, but published, and already on sale on Amazon and in many Angel and Holistic shops around the country. But that is exactly what happened! How? Through the most bizarre set of synchronicities! I can only conclude that when Spirit wants something done, it gets done! Obstacles? Problems? Difficulties? Not with Spirit!

The first set of synchronicities concerned the actual writing of the book, and getting started. Despite being told many times by various psychic friends that I was going to write a book, I really gave it no thought. There were, what you might call, a number of obstacles! Well, four, actually! First, what was I going to write about? Secondly, how was I going to get it published? I did not know anyone in the publishing business, or how to even go about finding a publisher! Thirdly, who was going to word-process it for me, whatever that "it" might be? Yes, I can word-process, but not for hours and hours on end. Spending all that time in front of a computer? Sorry! Not for me! Besides, I didn't even have a computer at that time! I have no difficulty in admitting that I really belong in carrier-pigeon days. And finally, where was I going to find outlets for this book? Major blockages to me, but of absolutely no significance to Spirit! Not even on the radar screen!

Do not be afraid! Follow your instincts! Go with the flow! See what happens!

I started to write. It began to flow. It wasn't automatic writing, but a flow of ideas and thoughts that literally funnelled through my head and arrived somehow on the page in front of me.

Within three hours of my starting to write, I had the introduction and list of contents sorted, publisher found, someone to word process it for me, and several outlets. How did that all happen? And within just three hours?

First, the subject matter of the book was already on paper, channelled through me by some unseen Force.

Secondly, how did I find a publisher?

I rang my good friend, Margaret Hurdman, spiritual medium, for our usual chat. When I mentioned, in joking, that I was writing a book, she just commented that it was near time, and immediately offered me the contact for her publisher, telling me to wait for about an hour before ringing him, to enable her to speak to him first on my behalf. Everything immediately moved so rapidly that I was literally caught up in a spiral from which I could not extricate myself. The publisher did not even ask me what I was writing about, (thank God for small mercies!), nor did I have the courage to tell him that I had just started an hour ago! To get the Christmas market, he would need my complete script sent to him within a few weeks. A few weeks! How could I? My Angels would have to work overtime to pull this one off!

Next problem! Who was going to word-process it for me? How was that going to materialise?

I had made an appointment with a friend of a friend for a psychic reading about a week previously, and to cut a long story short, the lady in question turned out to be a retired IT teacher! And our appointment really had not gone as planned! In fact, neither of us understood what it was all about. But Spirit did! Spirit had other plans for that meeting, and they had nothing to do with me getting a reading! Here was the answer to my word-processing problem!

 Three down, just one to go. Outlets? No problem to Spirit! I rang a few Angel shops where I was already known and a few where I was a total stranger, and each and every one agreed to retail for me. Now I was really committed! And the book not even on the horizon yet!

I continued to write, that same Force flowing through me down to my pen, and passed it all on for word-processing. It was just two weeks since I had first put pen to paper. My writing was finished!

Then the second set of synchronicities unfolded, this time concerning the front cover.

I had, just a few weeks previously, been attuned to Golden Eagle Reiki Healing (Native American), and had been joined by several Native American guides, whose presence I felt quite strongly around me. I had found a website, as I thought, by "accident", but which I now know was no such thing! Again, Spirit getting things done! I was already aware of White Eagle, but I had never read any of his books. So when his website popped up, I ordered some. The order arrived a few days later, and I left the box unopened, until after I had finished my writing.

Within a few more days, the publisher had the entire script, and sent me a few samples for the front cover. I knew what I wanted: a beautiful scene; a unicorn; a rainbow; an Angel and some Elementals. I picked the scene you can now see on the front cover of the book, and the rest were all added. Everything settled! Signed, sealed and confirmed!

I just had to wait now for my book to go on Amazon and for my first allocation to arrive.

I opened the box. I turned over the first book. I froze in disbelief, a chill going down my spine. The cover was the same scene I had chosen for my book! I began to read and was absolutely blown away by what I was reading in White Eagle's books. Just like what I had written!

Was I channelling White Eagle?

I still do not know, but Francesca Brown and Margaret Hurdman have both confirmed that I am channelling directly from the highest possible Source.

There is yet another synchronicity surrounding the cover. The tree in the foreground is the cherry tree in my own garden. How did it find its way onto the cover?

My trees are very precious to me. I connect with them all on a very deep level. This particular tree was holding on to its leaves, despite the fact that all the others had shed most of theirs. I was taking a photograph of the sun on the coloured leaves, and it suddenly struck me! The tree wanted to be in the book! I took the photo and immediately forwarded it on to be included. That night was a very calm Autumn night, no wind at all. Next morning, the tree was completely bare, all the leaves shed!

The cover of this present book is also built around a set of synchronicities. I have been recently drawn to unicorns, and without any input from me, the first sample of possible covers included a unicorn! Unicorns are a spiritual sign of raised awareness; an increase in spiritual consciousness. Very apt for the contents of this book! A black unicorn also signifies raised awareness, but in this case, that awareness is not yet identified or understood by the person concerned. Many people see black unicorns in a negative light, and are not as drawn to them as they would be to white unicorns, but black unicorns also bring protection. On this front cover, the white unicorn is bringing in the Divine Light through the opening behind; the stones represent grounding, the grounding of the Light; and the bell in the foreground is a Buddhist symbol, a symbol that we are being awakened to a new spiritual consciousness.

What have I learned from all this? I have learned that when we conquer our fears, by accepting that everything is happening for a reason and for our own highest good, trusting in Spirit, and going with our instincts, then the most amazing things happen; the most amazing synchronicities pour in. If I had listened to my fears and not gone with the flow, my book would never have materialised. How could it? To say it is my book is a misnomer. The book is from Spirit. I am only the conduit, the tool, the channel, whatever you wish to call it, as we all are, when Spirit wants something done.

I have witnessed the same thing happening while writing this, my second book. Only in this case, "Their" tactics have been different! Before I started writing the first book, I did not even know what I was going to write about. But once I started, the whole thing just materialised. This time, I did know what I was going to write about,- This Great Awakening; but I did not know how to go about it. And where did the information come from this time, to enable me to complete this book in just two weeks? Through my sleeping hours! The information seemed, somehow, to be pumped into me during my sleep. On wakening up every morning, for two whole weeks, I knew instinctively what I had to write. I had learned my lesson: let go and let God; do not be afraid! Take the leap of faith, the leap of trust in the Universe, and the Universe will respond!

Our fears are constantly being fed by the media, bombarding us daily with all the darker images of life on our Planet Earth, seldom the good. By placing so much emphasis on the negative, we are giving it credence, acknowledging its presence. And that negativity continues to increase our fears, in a vicious cycle. The past fills us with fears, likewise the future. If you are depressed, angry, resentful, you're living in the past. If you are fearful for the future, then you are living in the future. You cannot be fearful if you live in the present, because as you exist in the present moment, and can only do so, the past and future have no bearing on you, you have no fears! The more you try to live in the past or the future, the more you encourage and reinforce the subconscious, and consequently, the more you are controlled by fear.

Now, more and more people are accepting the challenge of freedom from controlling influences that imprisoned past generations. With time, most people will be drawn to love, rather than fear, which leads to hatred, killing and all forms of negativity.

Remember! What you send out, you get back. Your fears draw to you that which you fear. Your fear that your children will get ill, have an accident, or whatever, actually brings that on. Just trust that everything and everyone is being looked after by Divine Intelligence; worrying, fretting, fearing only impedes the flow of Divine goodness towards you. That is the meaning of Christ's words, "Do not be afraid!"

# Chapter 15

# The Sins of the Fathers

We generate our own reality; we create our own history; we freely choose our own actions. People on this earth have always generated the forces which are destined to manifest at a given time and place. The great prophets and seers of ancient times understood this completely; so completely that they were indeed able to foresee the future and predict when and how a nation was to rise or fall, when a civilization would reach a peak or a low point, when cataclysms were due, when major events would occur.

Today, our earth civilization is being shaken to its very foundations. Instability and uncertainty pervade and permeate every nation. And prophets and seers knew it would come about. How did they know? What knowledge did they possess to enable them to foretell accurately so much of what has indeed come about? Into what sources were they tapping?

The answer is that they did not, in fact, possess any particular extra powers at all. But what they were doing was acknowledging and accepting the 'Law of Karma', the foundation of many spiritual belief systems, known for thousands of years, and one of the most important of the Spiritual Laws of the Universe.

The Law of Karma has always, and continues, to trundle down through history, unstoppable, non-negotiable and unavoidable, just as night follows day, embodying and manifesting the simple theory of cause and effect, with karma being the effect side of it.

So, what is this force that we call the Law of Karma; this force to which we are all, each and every one of us, without exception, subjected?

The Law of Karma states that all our past actions determine our present reality, as well as our future circumstances. It can be expressed in several ways: what you give out, so you shall receive: as you sow, so shall you reap: do unto others as you would have them do unto you.

Everything is vibrating energy. Every thought, every word, every action, both past and present, creates a vibration that goes out into the Universe and attracts a similar vibration back to us. And whatever feelings, thoughts, words, your actions have caused in others, you will have exactly the same feelings, thoughts, actions, words returned to you

In these remarkable times in which we are now living, science, religion and spirituality are converging much more effectively and rapidly than ever before in the history of mankind. Newton's Third Law of Motion states that for every action, there is an equal and opposite reaction. This convergence of religion, spirituality, science, and mathematical expression of the Law of Karma does indeed auger well for humanity, because when it is fully understood and accepted in all educational areas, it will play a vital role in bringing peace and harmony to all peoples throughout the world, to all cultures and traditions, eradicating suffering, poverty and conflict. A magic elixir indeed!

So, how is this magic elixir going to establish itself in our psyche?

It is going to be generated through our understanding and acceptance of two fundamental basic Spiritual Laws of the Universe: firstly, we are all one, united spatially and lineally, there is no separation; and secondly, through the principle of Reincarnation. These two laws are fundamental to the Law of Karma.

We are responsible for our own actions and how they affect other people. We are not directly responsible for the choices other people make; we all have free will to determine our own actions. But we must be aware that how others are affected by our actions largely determines, in turn, their reactions. This is all part of the cyclical nature of things; the cycle of Karma, the wheel of Karma, and the cycle will continue to roll until it is broken.

There are two types of actions: good actions and bad actions. There are two types of Karma: good karma and bad karma. Good actions create good karma; bad actions create bad karma. Good actions and good karma contribute to future happiness; bad actions and bad karma bring about future unhappiness and suffering. Karma, therefore, is the basic foundation of absolutely everything in our lives.

Karma is not a punishment. And it is certainly not something imposed on us by God. God is not central to karma. What is central to karma is the acceptance of our personal responsibility for our own actions, words and thoughts. Punishment or retribution simply do not feature in any way, shape or form.

The Law of Karma is also bound up intrinsically with the Law of Reincarnation. Reincarnation is the repeated embodiment of a soul in physical bodies, on the basis of a linear time sequence, the aim of which is to provide souls with as many opportunities as they may need, to enable them to reach a certain stage of awareness or spiritual development. Karma is carried forward by each of us from lifetime to lifetime, until we learn that particular lesson; until we heal that particular situation or that particular relationship. If we do not experience the consequences of our actions in this particular life-time, it will carry through to a future life-time. There is no escape!

Once we have learned that particular lesson, then that particular karma, associated with that particular lesson, ends; we no longer carry that with us.

Lack of knowledge as to how the Law of Karma works, or indeed ignorance of its very existence, is what is holding humanity back. Ignorance enchains, imprisons and burdens us. Our education systems need to incorporate this Law of Karma into their teachings. Now, with the convergence of science, religion, spirituality and mathematics, this may happen. And when people understand, accept and embrace this law, they will be more circumspect about the thoughts, words and actions they send out. Happy days all around!

Karma is not just a personal, individual matter. It acts collectively as well as individually. And it is not just personal karma that needs clearing. Families, communities, countries, nations, all carry collective karma. The responsibility, not just of every individual and every person, but of every nation, is to be aware of the results of their respective actions, and also, indeed their lack of actions, their inaction, because in the inevitable course of time, these actions and inactions accumulate to form current conditions. Every nation, just like every individual, is responsible for its current conditions. And every government, just like every individual, is also accountable and responsible for its deeds. No one, absolutely no one, escapes karma!

The misery and suffering of any nation, people or race, is the direct result of the thoughts and actions of those who make up that race or nation. If the laws of harmony were violated in the past, then that harmony must be restored. There is no *"I"* or *"you"* in all of this; there is only the collective *"we"*. Every nation is responsible for the government that they themselves have voted into power. We are all connected; hence we are all responsible and accountable.

The Law of Karma is also bound up with our ancestors, our forefathers. Since some of our vibrations are entangled with some of our ancestors' vibrations, the past actions of our ancestors will also affect us. We carry with us DNA and genes from our ancestors, along with embedded wounds. What we are experiencing in our spiritual, emotional, mental and physical bodies, as well as all the traumas, difficulties, sufferings, successes, is what we and our ancestors have given out to others in the past. Yes! Karma is a combination of credits and debits, gathered up, permeating, seeping down through generations, until it is all balanced.

So, what does "Sins of the Fathers" mean? Does it mean that children are to be punished for the bad actions of their parents? No! Remember, there is no form of punishment, of any kind, inherent in the Law of Karma!

 Literature offers us many examples of personal and ancestral karma. Shakespeare's Romeo and Juliet, the *"star-crossed lovers"*, with their deaths, *"bury their parents' strife"*. Escalus, Prince of Verona, understands:

*"See what a scourge is laid upon your hate, / That heaven finds means to kill your joys with love. / And I for winking at your discords too / Have lost a brace of karma / All are punished."*

Capulet himself finally understands how the young lovers are *"poor sacrifices of our enmity"*. Tybalt, who lives by the sword and dies by the sword, is the epitome of hatred and violence. His hatred is the counterpart among the young, of Lady Capulet's extreme hatred among the old. We know exactly what kind of man Tybalt is when he first appears on stage, and with sword already drawn, says:

*"What, drawn and talk of peace? I hate the word / As I hate hell, all Montagues, and thee / Have at thee, coward!"*

Hatred, in Shakespeare's plays, as anywhere, is a violent and destructive force, a force which feeds upon itself and leads so many to the grave. And the young inherit from the old, just like in the old continuing family feud between the Montagues and the Capulets.

Karma is a recurrent theme throughout Shakespeare's plays. King Lear witnesses his words come back to haunt him; Macbeth gains no peace or contentment from murdering Duncan and usurping the throne. And! Here's the important bit! All of Scotland suffers for his misdeeds! And in "The Merchant of Venice", we hear:

*"The sins of the fathers are to be laid upon the children".*

William Blake, in his famous poem "Auguries of Innocence" warns us of the outcome if we harm or mistreat any other form of life:

*"Kill not the Moth nor Butterfly. / A dog starved at his Master's Gate / Predicts the ruin of the State / ..........A skylark wounded in the wing, / A Cherubim does cease to sing",* and how *"The wild deer, wandering here and there, / Keeps the Human Soul from care."*

Blake sees a *"World in a Grain of Sand",* and therefore cruelty, even to an ant, could shake the fabric of the Universe, being contrary to the Natural Law, which respects all life equally.

No! "Sins of the Fathers" does not mean that we are being punished for our ancestors' bad actions. Punishment infers a deity or Force dishing out some form of retaliatory action in return for what was done. There is no punishment meted out. "The sins of the Fathers" is simply a reference to the fact that as we sow, so shall we reap, and that applies spatially as well as lineally, with the emphasis being on the collective "we". Everything comes at a cost, not a punishment; everything has to be paid for; and future generations will pay the price for the bad actions of their ancestors. And yes! Bad karma always comes with a hefty price tag attached! That is the true meaning of "History repeats itself". Of course it does! And it will keep on repeating itself until the collective lessons are learned, and we get ourselves off the wheel of that particular karma!

And as far as the Law of Karma is concerned, the history books definitely need to be re-written!

What has gone down in History as glorious exploits, conquests and victories, have, and are still being paid for by us in today's world, and if we do not end the karma, future generations will continue to suffer from the back-lash. For example, what was seen as the glorious conquests of other countries in the struggle to enlarge empires by gaining colonies, has a much darker side to it. Those countries were not conquered or taken over in a spirit of love and friendship, but in a spirit of greed, a desire for personal gain, ambition and love of power. Those countries that were taken over did not gain anything or benefit in any way. They were exploited, plundered, pillaged, forced into service to the "Mother-Country", all for the conquerors' own gains. The old cliché, "the chickens come home to roost" certainly rings true in what is happening today with all the immigrants flooding Europe! Is that not karma for all that plundering and exploitation inflicted on those very same peoples centuries ago by the expanding powers of Europe? Is this not the children paying for the sins of the fathers?

Christopher Columbus and all the great explorers of the "glorious" Renaissance Age were hailed as heroes and adventurers of their time. But what did they bring to those new lands they discovered and claimed for their own? Wealth? Prosperity? Hardly! Only sickness and disease! Here was the start of expanding imperialism that culminated in the bad karma of World War One! The assassination of the Arch-Duke Franz Ferdinand and his wife at Sarajevo in 1914 only lit the bonfire that had been building up over centuries, in the mad, frantic scramble for overseas possessions and colonies. A build-up of bad karma indeed!

The displacement of indigenous peoples all over the world has caused misery and suffering on an untold scale, and they are still suffering. The Native Americans can no longer live their natural life-styles, close to Mother Nature, but now enclosed in reservations, bereft of their old ways of life, forced to abandon all they had and to live according to the dictates of others. How can that be justified? How can that possibly not create bad karma? But, it may well be the return of the Native American beliefs and spirituality on a large scale, that will save America from any further descent into a spiritual void.

The Aborigines! Suffering from all sorts of illnesses not of their own making! Diabetes; alcoholism; forced to adapt to Western food and Western life-styles, for which their bodies are not geared. Alice Springs; Darwin,- the Aborigines are there in their huge numbers, hanging about the streets, dependent on hand outs from the government, some people resenting the fact that their taxes are going to support them. Karma indeed for robbing these people of their lands and living!

In China, the one-child family policy is building up bad karma for China's future. All the abortions, pregnancy terminations; - that must all be balanced some day. And how will it be balanced? It will be balanced by a generation of selfish, self-orientated people, who have been denied the love of a sister or brother, and all the sharing and giving that goes with being part of a sibling family unit. Who is going to look after the old in a society where the words "brother" and "sister" do not even appear in the dictionary? And simply because they do not exist!

The U.S.A. consumes more than its fair share of world resources, and has interfered in many countries, not for their good, but for its own economic ambitions and greed. Big time! And American society has a huge gap between its rich and wealthy citizens on the one hand, and its destitute on the other. In balance, though, America does contribute to the welfare of poorer nations. That's some karma being paid back, at least!

The slave trade; the Industrial Revolution, with all its exploitation and suffering; world wars; - we are still feeling the effects of all of this. All this disharmony must be reversed, and then, and only then, will that bad karma end. Here in Ireland, a lot of bad karma was collected during the Celtic Tiger years, with the greed, grasping and materialism that swamped the country. The economic boom that erupted in Ireland would have been wonderful news if everyone had benefited. But that wasn't what happened! The gap between rich and poor widened, bringing extreme poverty and suffering to those on the lower end of the economic scale, while those on the upper range enjoyed amassing vast fortunes. Remember, we are all one! The wealthy in society have a responsibility towards the poorer members of that same society, in just the same way as richer nations have a responsibility towards the poorer countries. We are all one; we are all dependent on one another; there is no separation.

A lot of Ireland's bad karma was offset just recently, however, when the Irish people went to the polls and voted for equal rights for our Gay Community. That public display of tolerance, acceptance and unconditional love, in the face of both Church and Government opposition, certainly balanced a lot of Ireland's bad karma. It just showed how generous, open-hearted and compassionate the Irish people can be. As did the visit to Ireland, a few years ago, of Queen Elizabeth. The deep-rooted conflict between England and Ireland, going back over five hundred years; the resentment, the animosity, the desire for revenge, the hatred, the anger, all earned the nation of

Ireland bad karma. How can that be, you may well ask. How come Ireland collected bad karma, when it was England who committed the bad actions? And the answer to this one? - How we react to any event is within our own power, no one else can determine that. If we react with violence, then that is what we will get more of in return. See the cycle? The cycle of karma! Queen Elizabeth was welcomed warmly, and she publicly expressed regret and sorrow for what England had perpetrated on Ireland in the past. That's all it takes for bad karma to be dissolved: an apology in recognition of the wrongs that had been committed, and an acknowledgement of that apology. Likewise, President Obama's recent apology on behalf of the American people, for the wrongs inflicted on other nations by America in the past. Lesson learned! Clean slates all round!

The Ulster Plantation of Ireland by King James I of England ushered in a long period of animosity and hatred, for which we are still paying, many generations later. That hatred and resentment resurfaces every year during the so-called "marching season" in the Summer, with recurring conflicts over parades, flags, bands, each side vying for triumphalism. Yes, it is important to understand history, because only by understanding the past can we understand the present. But! We don't need to live there! We need to stop trying to get back at those who have harmed us in the past, and start healing the wounds. It matters not who fired the arrows; it matters only how we heal the wounds. Remember, how we react to the actions of others is our own choice, and by reacting to violence with more violence, we are only intensifying the amount of bad karma for future generations to come. We need to take on board the message and learn the lesson that no matter who has caused us pain, through irresponsibility, lack of accountability, narrowness of mind, ignorance,- we are all in this together, we are all one, and we all depend on each other. We have to end this ongoing cycle of collective karma, by accepting that living in a community, in a nation, in this world, means learning to share, not only the good, but also the pain and suffering as well, because one man's pain is every man's pain.

Someone needs to break the cycle! When we learn the lessons, all the karma will be swept away. We are not going to change the world in a day. Rid the world of gross materialism, war, famine, all in one day? Hardly! But, we can make a start! And where do I begin? With myself! See myself as Divine Essence, a portal for Divine Love and unity, and then spread that to others, one person at a time.

What else can we do? We can pray that our world leaders soon see the stupidity in spending all that money on weapons and ammunition to defend us from each other, and start to spend it instead on helping those in poverty and need. The only enemies of man are fear, guilt and anxiety. Not man himself! We are all one! How can you make an enemy of yourself? How can you want to kill yourself? How can you be envious of yourself?

The genetic memory of our families and our ancestors, which has been embedded in our DNA for seven generations, needs to be cleared. And the time to do it is now! There has never before been an opportunity, such as the opportunity we have now, at this particular point in time, with the present raising of the earth's vibration, to end the on-going cycle of bad karma. What someone does to you is what comes back to them; how you react is what comes back to you. How we react is our total responsibility. If we react with violence, we will only incur more of the same. Brilliant!!!!

By our actions today, we are forging the links that help or hinder our own progress, and that of all humanity in the future. Our human hearts must be changed first, and then reforms will follow. Reforms are useless, ineffective, without unconditional love behind them.

Only unconditional love can end the cycle of karma, can end the sons having to pay for the Sins of the Fathers.

# EPILOGUE

## We are being watched!

Are we the sole living organisms in a limitless and boundless cosmos? Are there any other forms of life out there? Are they like us? If so, why are they not making themselves known?

The search for signs of life beyond Planet Earth has taken astronomers to the far corners of the known Universe. And what we know about the Universe is very limited for two main reasons. Firstly, its vastness, its infinity; no corners, no boundaries, no limits. And secondly, we are seeing only through our human eyes, with limited and restricted vision.

Everything is Energy. We are energy, vibrating at a level sustainable on this Planet Earth. We need food; we need water; we need air. Fact! Indisputable! Without these, we would not exist! And by that I mean we would not exist in our present form. And we would certainly not exist on this particular dimension that is Planet Earth! But we would still exist! We would still exist in some other shape or form, in some other dimension, on some other energy vibration.

We know there is life in different dimensions: the Spirit World; the Celestial Kingdoms; the Elemental Kingdoms. We know too that Earth is the Planet with the most dense vibration; that is why it is such a desirable school for souls, affording greater opportunities to learn lessons that are not able to be learned in higher vibration dimensions. And why not? Simply because the lower based attributes such as greed, jealousy, self-ishness, ego, anger, do not exist on higher dimension levels of existence. We here on Earth have the monopoly on all of these. Charming! Those souls in existence on

119

other dimensions higher than that of Planet Earth operate only on Love, unconditional Love. That is all they know. They do not do war, violence, greed, hostility of any kind. They have progressed above that level. That is where we are heading too; but it will take some of us longer than others to get there, especially those of us still stuck in the lower Third Dimensions.

So of course we cannot expect to find life in any other part of the Galaxy similar to life here on Planet Earth. Conditions do not allow for it. But other, higher vibrational forms of life do not need what we need here on earth in order to exist! In the Spirit World, there is no necessity for food; no necessity for water; no necessity for air. And why not? Because there are no human physical bodies! Only our human physical bodies require all of those. As we progress up through the Spiritual ranks, we move to higher vibrational energy levels, and we continue in existence as higher, lighter vibrational forms of energy.

Earlier, I explained what happens when we arrive back with Spirit, if we find that our loved ones are on a higher vibrational level than us, then how do we ever get to visit them? We cannot ascend to their higher level, simply because we have not earned that level yet, but our loved ones on the higher vibrational level can descend to our lower level in order to facilitate a re-union. So too, in just the same way, we here on Planet Earth cannot access any form of higher vibration energy to make a connection with those on higher vibrational forms of energy, simply because we have not yet earned access to those higher levels. We have no business going there! That's the way it all works!

And that is exactly what is happening! They can see us, but we cannot see them; only when they allow us to see them! The raising of the Earth's vibration in 2012 has made us more accessible to them. They are watching us, not with intention to invade and conquer. War? Violence? Fear? Remember, we here on Earth have the monopoly on all of that! They come in peace and Love; that is all they know. And yes! Curiosity! Curiosity as to how we can behave in the way in which we are behaving; how we can kill and torture, steal and lie, cover up and manipulate, treat each other in the way we do. They are looking at us in awe, wonder and amazement and perhaps, too, apprehension, that maybe, just maybe, we might launch a nuclear weapon that will destroy not only what we have left to destroy of Planet Earth, but also other parts of the entire Universe, because, remember, everything in the entire Cosmos, all forms of life, human, vegetable, mineral, we are all connected in the great flow of Universal Divine Energy. What affects one, affects all!

The forms of life that exist on these higher vibrational energy waves are so far advanced from us on their Spiritual path that we cannot imagine the advanced technology or the mental powers they have. Telepathy, kinesiology, mind control, tele-porting,- these are all part of their existence! We are all on our long walk-about across Eternity, and they are millions of Light years ahead of us. But we are all going in the same direction, and we too will exist in similar circumstances to them when we have earned that higher vibrational frequency.

Science continues to search for life in Space, but that life will only be found on different energy frequency waves, not in tangible forms of life as we know it.

James Cameron's movie "Avatar" may indeed be much nearer the truth than many of us are prepared to believe. I wonder who or what is inspiring him? What higher-vibrational influence is working on James Cameron, instilling into his mind, inspiring him to reveal to humanity, at this point in time in This Great Awakening, what needs to be revealed to us, telling us what we need to know? Perhaps the time has come, perhaps the time is now for us to receive a friendly hand from somewhere out there, a hand offering unconditional Love, to assist us in This Great Awakening Process, rescuing us from the depths into which we have sunk, raising us up to realise that we are all One, we are all of Divine Essence and we can all live in peace and harmony.

At least think about it!

Made in the USA
Charleston, SC
21 September 2015